Contents

KU-264-940

Macmillan Literature Collections

Welcome to the *Macmillan Literature Collections* – a series of advanced level readers containing original, unsimplified short stories written by famous classic and modern writers. We hope that these stories will help to ease the transition from graded readers to reading authentic novels.

Each collection in the series includes:

Introduction
- an introduction to the short story
- tips for reading authentic texts in English
- a carefully-chosen selection of classic and modern short stories.

The stories
Each story is presented in three parts: the introduction and pre-reading support material; the story; and post-reading activities. Each part includes the following sections:
- *About the author* – in-depth information about the author and their work
- *About the story* – information about the story, including background information about setting and cultural references
- *Summary* – a brief summary of the story that does not give away the ending.

Pre-reading activities
- *Key vocabulary* – a chance to look at some of the more difficult vocabulary related to the main themes and style of the story before reading the story
- *Main themes* – a brief discussion of the main themes, with questions to keep in mind as you read.

The story
You will find numbered footnotes in the stories. These explain cultural and historical references, and key words that you will need to understand the text. Many of these footnotes give definitions of words which are very formal, old-fashioned or rarely used in modern English. You will find more common, useful words and phrases from the stories in the *Glossary* at the end of the book. Words included in the *Glossary* will appear in **bold**.

Post-reading activities

- *Understanding the story* – comprehension questions that will help you make sure you have understood the story
- *Language study* – a section that presents and practises key linguistic and structural features of authentic literary texts (you will find an index of the areas covered at the end of the book)
- *Literary analysis* – discussion questions that guide you to an in-depth appreciation of the story, its structure, its characters and its style.

In addition, at the end of each book there are:
- suggested *Essay questions*
- a comprehensive *Glossary* highlighting useful vocabulary from each story
- an index for the *Language study* section.

In *Food Stories*, there are recipes for the dishes from the stories.

How to use these books

You can use these books in whatever way you want. You may want to start from the beginning and work your way through. You may want to pick and choose. The *Contents* page gives a very brief, one-line introduction to each story to help you decide where to start. You may want to learn about the author and the story before you read each one, or you may prefer to read the story first and then find out more about it afterwards. Remember that the stories and exercises can be challenging, so you may want to spend quite a long time studying each one. The most important thing is to enjoy the collection – to enjoy reading, to enjoy the stories and to enjoy the language that has been used to create them.

Answer keys

In many cases you can check your answers in the story by using the page references given. However, an Answer key for all the exercises is available at www.macmillanenglish.com/readers.

Introduction

What is a short story?

A short story is shorter than a novel, but longer than a poem. It is usually between 1,000 and 20,000 words long. It tells a story which can usually be read quite quickly. It often concentrates on one, central event; it has a limited number of characters, and takes place within a short space of time.

History of the short story

Stories and storytelling have existed for as long as people have had language. People love, and need, stories. They help us explain and understand the world. Before people could read or write, story tellers travelled from village to village, telling stories.

The first written stories developed from this storytelling tradition. Two of the best known examples of early, written stories in Europe appeared in the 14th century. Chaucer's *Canterbury Tales* and Bocaccio's *Decameron* are both based on the same idea. A group of people who are travelling or living together for a short time, agree to tell each other stories. Their individual short stories are presented together as one long story.

The first modern short stories appeared at the beginning of the 19th century. Early examples of short story collections include the *Fairy Tales* (1824–26) of the Brothers Grimm, and Edgar Allan Poe's *Tales of the Grotesque and Arabesque* (1840). In the late 19th century, printed magazines and journals became very popular and more and more short stories were published. By the 20th century most well-known magazines included short stories in every issue and the publishers paid a lot of money for them. In 1952 Ernest Hemingway's short story, *The Old Man and the Sea*, helped sell more than five million copies of the magazine *Life* in just two days.

The short story today

Today, short stories are often published in collections called anthologies. They are usually grouped according to a particular category – by theme, topic, national origin, time or author. Some newspapers and magazines continue to print individual stories. Many short stories are first published on the Internet, with authors posting them on special-interest websites and in online magazines.

Reading authentic literary texts in English

Reading authentic literary texts can be difficult. They may contain grammatical structures you have not studied, or expressions and sayings you are not familiar with. Unlike graded readers, they have not been written for language students. The words have been chosen to create a particular effect, not because they are easy or difficult. But you do not need to understand every word to understand and enjoy the story. When you are reading in your own language you will often read so quickly that you skip over words and read for the general effect, rather than the details. Try to do the same when you are reading in English. Remember that stopping to look up every word you don't know slows you down and stops you enjoying the story.

When you are reading authentic short stories, remember:
– It should be a pleasure!
– You should read at your own pace.
– Let the story carry you along – don't worry about looking up every word you don't understand.
– Don't worry about difficult words unless they stop you from understanding the story.
– Try not to use the *Glossary* or a dictionary when you're reading.

You might want to make a note of words to look up later, especially key words that you see several times (see *Using a Dictionary* on page 9 for more tips on looking up and recording new words). But remember, you can always go back again when you have finished the story. That is the beauty of reading short stories – they are short! You can finish one quite quickly, especially if you do not worry about understanding every single word; then you can start again at the beginning and take your time to re-read difficult passages and look up key words.

Preparing yourself for a story

It is always a good idea to prepare yourself, mentally, before starting a story.
– Look at the title. What does it tell you about the story? What do you expect the story to be about?
– If there is a summary, read it. This will help you follow the story.
– Quickly read the first few paragraphs and answer these questions: Where is it set?

When is it set?

Who is the main character?

– As you read, concentrate on following the gist (the general idea) of the story. You can go back and look at the details later. You can use the questions at the end of the story (see *Understanding the story*) to help you make sure you understand what is happening.

Tips for dealing with difficult passages

Some stories include particularly difficult passages. They are usually descriptive and give background information, or set the scene. They are generally difficult to follow because they are full of specific details. Try to read these passages quickly, understanding what you can, and then continue with the story. Make a note of the passage and come back to it later, when you have finished the whole story.

If, at any time, you are finding it difficult to follow the story, go back to this difficult passage. It may hold the answers to your questions.

Read through the passage again carefully and underline all the unknown words. Try to understand as much as you can from the immediate context and what you now know about the story. Then, look up any remaining words in the *Glossary* at the back of the book, or in your dictionary.

Tips for dealing with difficult words

– Decide if the word (or phrase) is important to the overall message. Read the whole paragraph. Do you understand the general meaning? Yes? Then the word isn't important. Don't worry about it. *Keep reading!*

– If you decide the word is important, see if you can work out its meaning from the context. Is it a verb, a noun or an adjective? Is it positive or negative? What word would you translate it into in your language? Underline it or make a note of it and the page number, but *keep reading*. If it really is an important word, you will see it again.

– If you keep seeing the same word in the story, and you still can't understand it, look in your monolingual dictionary!

Using a dictionary

Looking up words

Before you look up the word, look at it again in its context. Decide what part of speech it is. Try to guess its meaning from the context. Now look it up in your dictionary. There may be more than one definition given. Decide which one is the most appropriate. If the word is something very specific, e.g. the name of a flower or tree, you may want to use a bilingual dictionary to give you the exact translation.

Let's look at how this works in practice. Look at this short extract and follow the instructions below.

> ... there is a little valley or rather **lap** of land among high hills, which is one of the quietest places in the whole world. A small **brook** glides through it, with just murmur enough to **lull** one to repose*
>
> *literary: *sleep or rest*
> *The Legend of Sleepy Hollow* by Washington Irvine

1 Look at the words in bold and decide what part of speech they are – noun, verb, adjective, etc.
2 Try to guess what it might mean.
3 Look at the extracts below from the *Macmillan English Dictionary for Advanced Learners*. Choose the most appropriate definition.

Words with more than one entry Sometimes the same word belongs to more than one word class: for example, **brook** can be both a noun and a verb. Each word class is shown as a separate entry. The small number at the end of the head-word tells you that a word has more than one entry.	**brook¹** noun a small river **brook²** verb **not brook** – to definitely not allow or accept something **lap¹** noun **1** the top half of your legs above your knees when you sit down **2** one complete turn around a course in a race PHRASE in the lap of luxury in very comfortable and expensive conditions **lap²** verb **1** if an animal laps water, it drinks it gently with its tongue
Idioms and fixed expressions Some words are often used in idioms and fixed expressions. These are shown at the end of the entry, following the small box that says PHRASE.	**lull¹** noun a quiet period during a very active or violent situation **lull²** verb **1** to make someone feel relaxed and confident so that they are not prepared for something unpleasant to happen: *their report lulled us into a false sense of security*
Words with more than one meaning Many words have more than one meaning, and each different meaning is shown by a number.	**2** to make someone relaxed enough to go to sleep

Dictionary extracts adapted from the Macmillan English Dictionary 2nd Edition © Macmillan Publishers Limited 2007 *www.macmillandictionary.com*

Keeping a record

When you have looked in your dictionary, decide if the word is interesting or useful to you. If it is, make a note of it, and write down its definition. Make a note of the sentence where you found it in the story, then write one or two more examples of your own. Only do this for those words you think you will need to use in the future.

Here is an example of how you might record the word *lull*.

> 'with just murmur enough to <u>lull</u> one to repose'
>
> <u>Lull</u> – to make you feel relaxed enough to go to sleep
>
> e.g. The quiet sound of the waves lulled me to sleep
>
> The mother sang to her baby to lull it to sleep

Literary analysis

The *Literary analysis* section is written to encourage you to consider the stories in more depth. This will help you to appreciate them better and develop your analytical skills. This section is particularly useful for those students who are studying, or intending to study, literature in the medium of English. Each section includes literary terms with which you may or may not be familiar.

Macmillan Readers website

For more help with understanding these literary terms, and to find Answer keys to all the exercises and activities, visit the Macmillan Readers website at www.macmillanenglish.com/readers. There you will also find a wealth of resources to help your language learning in English, from listening exercises to articles on academic and creative writing.

An Old-Fashioned Thanksgiving

by Louisa May Alcott

About the author

Louisa May Alcott was a popular nineteenth-century American novelist. She is best known as a writer for children, although her work has remained an influence on adults up to the present day. When her most celebrated novel, *Little Women*, came out in 1868, it was an instant success, selling in the United States and abroad. One reviewer wrote that it was 'the very best of books to reach the hearts of the young of any age from six to sixty'. Since then, it has never been out of print. The story is a family saga which follows the lives of four sisters as they grow up, leave home and get married. Much of the plot is autobiographical, mirroring Alcott's own varied and difficult life.

Alcott was born in what is now Pennsylvania, in the north-eastern United States, in 1832, the second of four daughters. Her father was a teacher and a transcendentalist – someone who believed that people should try to become independent from society. He taught the young Louisa to work hard towards the ideal of personal perfection – an impossible goal for any child, and one that she struggled with as she grew up.

In 1838, the family moved to Boston, where her father tried to establish a school based on transcendentalist principles. Living in and around Boston at this time were several of the most influential writers and thinkers of the time, some of whom were also transcendentalists. They included Henry Thoreau and Ralph Waldo Emerson, who remain central figures in American literature today, and they played a part in Alcott's unusual education and upbringing. The school faced difficulties, so the Alcotts moved to a rented cottage in a village called Concord. Here the four girls enjoyed an idyllic rural childhood and were very happy. Orchard Cottage, as it is still known today, later became the fictional home for the sisters in *Little Women*.

Louisa May Alcott, like Jo, the main character in *Little Women*, enjoyed doing things traditionally limited to men. Unusually for a woman in those days, she had a busy professional life. The family was educated but poor, and the girls were encouraged to earn money, contrary to the traditional belief that women should be financially dependent on men. Alcott started her working life as a teacher when she was just sixteen. Later, during the Civil War, although she could not fight, she volunteered as a nurse. She believed in women's right to vote and was the first woman in her town to register to do so. Her feminism was intensely personal. She once wrote: 'I am more than half-persuaded that I am a man's soul put ... into a woman's body', and it is certainly true that she refused to let the fact that she was a woman limit her. Alcott never married. Her only known romantic relationship was with a Polish man she met when travelling in Switzerland.

While she was a nurse during the Civil War, she contracted typhoid fever. Sadly, the medicine used to treat her gave her mercury poisoning, and for the rest of her life she suffered regular illness and pain. In 1863 she wrote *Hospital Sketches*, based on her letters home from the war, and this became her first best seller. From this point on her writing career took off. During the 1860s she wrote sensational and dramatic novels for adults under a different name, A.M. Barnard, but it wasn't until 1868 that she became well known under her own name, when *Little Women* was published. This new novel was different from the books she had written under the name of Barnard. It focused less on dramatic stories and more on social themes. It was followed by the sequels *Good Wives*, *Little Men* and finally, in 1886, *Jo's Boys*.

She wrote many books, poems and short stories from the 1860s until her death in 1888, often about girls and young women growing up and struggling with the difficulties of life. Her themes of education, the importance to society of family love and women's changing roles in society were extremely relevant to her readers in the past and her works are still popular today. She is buried in the cemetery in Concord, on a hillside called 'Authors' Ridge', next to other great American writers.

About the story

Louisa May Alcott wrote *An Old-Fashioned Thanksgiving* in 1881 as part of a series of collections of short stories known as *Aunt Jo's Scrap Bag* that she wrote over a ten-year period.

Background information

Food in the story

The food in the story is related to Thanksgiving, a national holiday in the United States celebrated each November. Its origins go back to 1621 when the very first Europeans settled in North America. They were called the Pilgrims. These were groups of people who had suffered religious hatred in England and had come to the 'New World' in search of religious freedom. The first few years on the new continent were very hard. They planted crops to grow food, but the results weren't always successful. In autumn, when they collected the crops and saw that the harvest was good, they celebrated with a large meal and prayers of thanks. Games were played and people danced to folk music played on the fiddle (violin).

George Washington, the first president of the United States, made Thanksgiving a national holiday in 1789. In Louisa May Alcott's time, President Lincoln fixed the date of Thanksgiving as the last Thursday in November, and ever since that day in 1863 it has remained the same.

Thanksgiving is a time for families to come together to eat. Typically, the meal consists of a turkey, which is larger than a chicken and can feed lots of people. It is served with potatoes and other autumn vegetables such as squash and pumpkin. The turkey is roasted in the oven and filled with a mixture of bread and onion called *stuffing*, which is flavoured with herbs such as sage, summer savoury or marjoram. The turkey is tied up with string, or *yarn*, to stop the stuffing falling out.

While it is cooking, the meat is kept from drying out by *basting* it, which means regularly pouring fatty liquids from the cooking over it. It is often accompanied by cranberry sauce, a type of fruit jam.

Many rich foods containing lots of sugar are eaten at this time. Mince pies are sweet pies filled with dried fruit and spices. Plum pudding is the traditional dessert at Thanksgiving; it is made from fruits such as apples, dates, raisins and oranges, spices and animal fat called *suet*.

There is a recipe for roast turkey with stuffing on page 188.

The work ethic

Life was hard in the countryside at the time the story is set (the 1820s). Running a farm and feeding a family was hard work. Rural families like the one in the story believed that it was morally important to be a hard-working member of your society and family. From the oldest to the youngest, all were expected to help with the household chores, such as cooking, cleaning and collecting wood. The house was the responsibility of the women and girls, while the men and older boys took charge outside around the farm. In the evenings, the women made clothes by spinning wool, knitting, sewing or doing decorative embroidery, while the boys whittled wood – making wooden objects by shaping pieces of wood with a small knife.

Not only was it important to use one's time well, but being poor also meant that it was necessary to be thrifty – to make good use of everything you had and not waste it. It showed a lack of respect to throw away what nature offered.

The hearth

The hearth was the name given in the past to the kitchen fireplace, where food was cooked, water heated and the whole house warmed. It was so central to the life of the house that the word *hearth* is sometimes used poetically as a metaphor for the soul of the house. Much of the action in the story takes place around the hearth.

Summary

It may help you to know something about what happens in the story before you read it. Don't worry, this summary does not tell you how the story ends!

The Bassett family is a large family. There are eight children. The oldest is sixteen and the youngest is a baby. They live on a farm in Pennsylvania. Winter is approaching, and the family is busy preparing for Thanksgiving. Normally the family goes to their grandmother's house to spend the holiday with their cousins, but since she is unwell, they have decided to stay on the farm. Mrs Bassett is at the centre of all this activity. She is in the kitchen, cooking and planning the meals, while at the same time making sure that everyone has something to do.

They have an unexpected visitor, who has a message from a neighbour of their grandmother's. He tells them that her health is getting worse and that they should come straight away. Without any delay, Farmer Bassett and his wife prepare for the twenty-mile journey through the snow, on a sleigh pulled by their horse. They take the baby with them and leave the oldest children, Eph and Tilly, in charge of the farm and of the younger children until their father returns the following evening.

The children enjoy their new responsibilities, and the oldest children Eph, sixteen, and Tilly, fourteen, take on their roles as the adults with enthusiasm. A snowstorm starts outside, but the children are all safe and happy indoors. Tilly prepares lunch and after that the children enjoy a variety of activities indoors.

After supper, Eph reads the children a story from a history book before they go to bed. The storm continues outside. The following morning, the two oldest girls, Tilly and Prue, turn their attention to the Thanksgiving dinner that had been planned. They decide that the meal should go ahead, even though their mother is not there and they have never prepared such a complicated meal before. Unsure of the exact ingredients, they do their best and are quite happy with their efforts.

Everything is ready: the table is laid and the children are waiting for their father to come home. Just then, a less welcome visitor is seen slowly approaching the house.

Pre-reading activities

Key vocabulary

This section will help you familiarize yourself with some of the more specific vocabulary used in the story. You may want to use it to help you before you start reading, or as a revision exercise after you have finished the story.

Food and cooking

Most of the action in the story takes place in the kitchen. Here is some of the key vocabulary used to describe the kitchen, the cooking equipment and the ingredients.

1 **Read the description below of a museum exhibition showing a farmhouse kitchen from the time of the story and match the words in bold with their definitions (a–m).**

   The old farmhouse kitchen was a perfect copy. There were **garlands** of dried apples, onions and corn hanging on the wall. Above them, hanging from the roof, there were **squashes** and dry **venison**, which came from the deer that they hunted in the forests around the farm. On a **crane** over the fire there were steaming **kettles** and down in the red **embers** of the fire, copper **saucepans** sat, all caught in the moment of preparing a special feast.

   A life-like model of a farmer's wife wearing a white **apron** was putting the long **spit** into its position on the tall **andirons**, while her daughter put the **dripping pan** underneath in preparation for roasting the meat. At a table another young girl was putting spices into a **mortar** and a third was cutting meat with a **chopper.**

a) a bowl in which you crush substances into a powder using a tool called a pestle
b) a strong metal structure used for hanging heavy pots over the fire
c) metal supports that hold wood burning in a fireplace, normally with vertical posts used to stop the wood from falling out
d) a container that is used for boiling water
e) a metal tray used to catch the fat that falls from roasting meat
f) a long, sharp piece of metal used for holding and turning meat as it cooks over a fire
g) a piece of wood or coal that is still hot and red even after a fire has stopped burning

h) something that you wear to protect your clothes, especially when you are cooking
i) a round, deep metal container with a long handle, used for cooking food
j) a heavy knife with a large, square blade for cutting meat
k) the meat from a deer
l) dried fruit or vegetables hanging on a piece of string (also used to describe a ring of flowers or leaves used for decoration)
m) a large, hard vegetable with very thick skin

The story is about the preparation of a big meal and the process of cooking it is described in detail.

2 **Read the verbs and their definitions and the three words or expressions that follow. In each case one word or expression cannot be used with that verb. Which one?**

1 **chop** cut food into smaller pieces
   meat / potato / honey

2 **grind** break food, such as herbs or garlic, into very small pieces or powder, by crushing it between two hard surfaces
   the spices / the juice / the pepper

3 **knead** prepare dough (uncooked bread) by pressing it continuously with your hands
   an apple / the biscuit mixture / the uncooked pizza base

4 **mash** press food, often already cooked, so hard that it breaks into very small pieces and forms a kind of paste
   the boiled potatoes / an avocado / the herbs

5 **peel** remove the skin from a fruit or vegetable
   a pear / some sauce / a potato

6 **pop** move something quickly to a particular position
   the potatoes in the saucepan / the table / the meat in the oven

7 **pound** hit something hard many times so that it breaks into small pieces
   the dry ingredients / the spices / the bread

8 **shell** remove the outer part that covers nuts, peas or other foods
   corn / meat / peanuts

9 **slice** cut something into thin pieces
   the meat / some bread / the milk

10 **stir** move liquid around in a dish or pan using a spoon
   the turkey / the sauce / the milk

Features of a farmhouse

Most of the story is set indoors in the old Bassett family farmhouse. Old-fashioned names for the various rooms and furniture are used.

3 Read the words and definitions below and choose the correct words to complete the paragraph that follows.

> **barn** a large building on a farm where animals, crops or machines are kept
> **beam** a long, thick piece of wood, metal or concrete that supports a roof
> **bin** a large container used for storing food (in modern usage for storing rubbish)
> **buttery** a room for storing food, usually next to the kitchen
> **cellar** a room under a building, below the level of the ground
> **dresser** a large piece of furniture with drawers and cupboards underneath and a flat, wide workspace for preparing food on top, often with shelves at the back
> **garret** a very basic room just under the roof of a house
> **parlor** a room in a house, used for entertaining guests (*British spelling*: parlour)
> **settle** a long wooden bench, with a tall, straight back and arms, often with a chest underneath
> **sitting room** another name for the living room
> **yard** an enclosed area around a building where people can do activities outside

There was so much food from that year's harvest that there was not the smallest space for any more in the farmhouse. The (1) *bins/dressers/beams* outside in the (2) *yard/garret/cellar* were full of wheat from the fields and the fruit and vegetables were kept down in the (3) *garret/cellar/sitting room* where it was cool and dark. Hanging from the (4) *bins/barns/beams* in the kitchen were all sorts of food: herbs, strings of onions, even a rabbit. It had even been necessary to store dry food upstairs in the (5) *yard/garret/parlor*. The children were all busy. Tilly was in the kitchen chopping vegetables on the (6) *dresser/settle/garret*, while Prue was in the (7) *buttery/beam/dresser* looking for onions. The younger children had been told not to go into the (8) *beam/parlor/settle* but to stay in the (9) *dresser/sitting room/bin*, where they sat on the (10) *buttery/settle/beam*, playing calmly. Eph was outside in the (11) *sitting room/cellar/barn*, feeding the cows.

Adverbs of manner

Adverbs add detail to the way the people act in the story, and tell us a great deal about the emotions behind their actions.

4 Read the adverbs and their definitions below. Use them to complete the sentences.

boldly in a confident way and showing no fear
briskly quickly and energetically
devoutly in a way that shows strong religious belief or feeling
drowsily in a way that shows you want to sleep
hastily in a hurry because you do not have much time
luxuriously in a way that shows someone is enjoying a very pleasant, comfortable or relaxing situation
nobly behaving in an honest and brave way that other people admire
quaintly in a way that is interesting or attractive with a slightly strange and old-fashioned quality
tenderly in a gentle way that shows that you care about someone or something

1 They worked fast at their chores, Tilly .... preparing the spices.
2 Tilly stood .... at the door, ready to block the wild animal should it try to enter.
3 Prue wanted to make her sister happy and whispered .... to her not to worry.
4 Seth .... put on his shoes to follow the boys outside but left his laces undone.
5 The picture showed two .... dressed children from the sixteenth century.
6 Eph prayed .... that the children would do no damage.
7 Both girls felt responsible for the mistake, but Prue .... took the blame.
8 The dog lay in front of the fire, ... warming his legs.
9 It was late; the younger children cuddled up .... to one another in their beds.

Adjectives describing physical health

Country living is clearly a healthy way of life for the Bassetts, as the words Alcott uses to describe them suggests.

5 Read the adjectives and their definitions in the box. Which would you associate with:

a) boys?
b) girls?
c) a woman?
d) any of the above?

> **bold** confident and not afraid of people
> **buxom** fat in an attractive way
> **hardy** strong and able to deal with or exist in unpleasant or extreme conditions
> **hearty** friendly and enthusiastic
> **plump** slightly fat with a rounded shape, often used in a pleasant way
> **rosy** pink and looking healthy
> **stout** brave or sturdy; can also mean slightly fat
> **sturdy** strong and not easily hurt, damaged or affected by what happens

When you have read the story, come back and check your answers.

Expressions of happiness

The Bassett family are a happy family and this is reflected in the language of the story.

6 **Read the extracts. Decide if the words and expressions in bold (1–11) are nouns, verbs, adjectives or adverbs. Then match them with their definitions below (a–k).**

*Tilly pulled his hair, and the story ended with a general (1) **frolic***

*Eph took his fiddle and scraped away (2) **to his heart's content** in the parlor*

*Tilly laughed, and all the rest joined in, so (3) **good humor** was restored*

*He stood on his hind legs, and seemed to sniff (4) **with relish** the savory odors that poured out of the window.*

*"If that is a funeral, the mourners are uncommonly (5) **jolly**," said Eph, dryly, as merry voices and loud laughter broke the white silence without.*

*"Oh, my patience! Ain't I glad I got dinner, and don't I hope it will turn out good!" exclaimed Tilly, while the twins (6) **pranced** with delight, and the small boys roared:*

"Hooray for Pa! Hooray for Thanksgivin'!"

*The (7) **cheer** was answered (8) **heartily**, and in (they) came …, all (9) **in great spirits**; and all much surprised to find such a (10) **festive** welcome.*

*lively games soon set everyone (11) **bubbling over** with jollity,*

a) a good mood
b) a loud shout of happiness or approval
c) as much or as often as you like
d) connected with a festival or celebration
e) friendly and cheerful
f) if a happy or excited feeling does this, you feel it very strongly and usually show that you are feeling it
g) in a loud or enthusiastic way
h) in a very good mood
i) walk or move in a lively confident way that may seem silly or annoying to other people
j) a happy, lively game or activity
k) with great pleasure and satisfaction

Colloquial speech

The rural American dialect of the characters in the story is quite different from standard American English. Alcott writes the direct speech as it would have sounded, with its own special vocabulary, accent and even grammar.

Vocabulary

In the extract below, it is possible to guess that *critters* is a synonym of *cattle* (cows) from the context. It also looks like the word *creatures*.

> "Now, Eph, you must look after the **cattle** like a man and keep up the fires, for there's a storm brewin', and' neither the children nor dumb **critters** must suffer," said Mr. Bassett.

7 **Read the words and their definitions. Which words can you guess the meaning of just by looking at them?**

chorin' doing chores such as cleaning and collecting wood
coast walk without a particular purpose or direction
critters creatures, animals
darst dare
drove rushed or hurried
dubersome doubtful
jog hurry up
lonesome unhappy because you are alone or because you have no friends
'Sakes alive!' interjection used for saying that you are surprised
semintary cemetery
yonder *old-fashioned:* used for talking about someone or something that is not near you, e.g. 'Look over yonder'

Accent

8 Read the words from both lists out loud. Try to imagine how the words in the second list are pronounced. What differences in vowel pronunciation do you notice? What other differences are there?

Standard English	Rural American dialect
just	jest
dozen	dezzen
sitting room	settin-room
if	ef
mercy	marcy
herbs	yarbs
steady	stiddy
boiled	biled
daughter	darter
hollow	holler
worse	wuss
china	chiny
Thanksgiving	Thanksgivin'
starving	starvin'
less than	less'n
them	'em
kept up	kep' up
picture	picter

9 Match the words (1–10) to their standard English equivalents (a–j).

1	'fore	a)	getting
2	buffalers	b)	pudding
3	extry	c)	stomach
4	fust	d)	before
5	gittin'	e)	extra
6	jedge	f)	first
7	puddin'	g)	buffalo
8	sence	h)	since
9	stomick	i)	weren't
10	warn't	j)	judge

Grammar

Look at the following sentences from the story and their equivalents in standard English.

1 *Don't it look nice?*	Doesn't it look nice?
2 *I ain't afeared.*	I'm not afraid.
3 *It don't come but once a year.*	It only comes once a year.
4 *I'm dreadful sorry.*	I'm dreadfully sorry.
5 *I couldn't cook nor eat no way now.*	I couldn't cook or eat anyway now.

10 Which of the sentences above contains:

a) an adjective being used as an adverb?

b) a double negative?

c) a non-standard negative?

d) an unusual use of 'but'?

e) a non-standard subject-verb agreement?

American spelling

The story is written in American English. Here are some of the basic spelling differences you'll find.

1 *our* ➜ *or* : honour/honor, parlour/parlor, colour/color, savoury/savory, odour/odor, humour/humor, vigour/vigor

2 *s* ➜ *z* : cosy/cozy

3 dropping the final *e*: axe/ax

4 not doubling consonants: woollen/woolen

Main themes

Before you read the story, you may want to think about some of its main themes. The questions will help you think about the story as you are reading it for the first time. There is more discussion of the main themes in the *Literary analysis* section after the story.

Family

The story concerns a large family and focuses on the relationships between the children and between the parents and the children.

11 As you read the story, think about the following questions:

a) What kind of family is it? Does it have anything in common with your family or other families that you know of?

b) What responsibilities are the children given? How do the children react to these responsibilities?

Gender roles

The story describes in detail many of the traditional aspects of domestic life, such as cooking, cleaning, looking after children and old people and protecting the family from danger. The family home is also a working farm with animals and land to take care of, so there is a lot to do.

12 As you read the story, ask yourself:

a) Who is responsible for the work in the house?

b) Would you rather be a boy or a girl in this family? Why?

An Old-Fashioned Thanksgiving

by Louisa May Alcott

SIXTY YEARS AGO, up among the New Hampshire hills, lived Farmer Bassett, with a houseful of sturdy sons and daughters growing up about him. They were poor in money, but rich in land and love, for the wide acres[1] of wood, corn, and **pasture** land fed, warmed, and clothed the **flock**, while mutual patience, affection, and courage made the old farmhouse a very happy home.

November had come; the crops were in, and barn, buttery, and bin were overflowing with the harvest that rewarded the summer's hard work. The big kitchen was a jolly place just now, for in the great fireplace roared a cheerful fire; on the walls hung garlands of dried apples, onions, and corn; up aloft[2] from the beams shone crook-necked squashes, juicy hams, and dried venison – for in those days deer still haunted the deep forests, and hunters flourished. Savory smells were in the air; on the crane hung steaming kettles, and down among the red embers copper saucepans simmered, all suggestive of some approaching feast.

A white-headed baby lay in the old blue cradle that had rocked six other babies, now and then lifting his head to look out, like a round, full moon, then subsided to kick and crow[3] contentedly, and suck the rosy apple he had no teeth to bite. Two small boys sat on the wooden settle shelling corn for popping, and picking out the biggest nuts from the goodly[4] store their own hands had gathered in October. Four young girls stood at the long dresser, busily chopping meat, pounding spice, and slicing apples; and the tongues of Tilly, Prue, Roxy, and Rhody went as fast as their

1 a unit for measuring the surface area of land
2 *literary:* high up in the air
3 *old-fashioned:* if a baby crows, it makes a sound that shows it is happy
4 *old-fashioned*: a large number or amount

hands. Farmer Bassett, and Eph, the oldest boy, were "chorin'
'round" outside, for Thanksgiving was **at hand**, and all must be
in order for that time-honored day.

To and fro, from table to hearth, **bustled** buxom Mrs. Bassett,
flushed and floury, but busy and blithe[5] as the queen bee of this
busy little **hive** should be.

"I do like to begin seasonable and have things to my mind.
Thanksgivin' dinners can't be drove, and it does take a sight of
victuals[6] to fill all these hungry stomicks," said the good woman,
as she gave a vigorous stir to the great kettle of cider applesauce,
and cast a **glance** of housewifely pride at the fine **array** of pies set
forth on the buttery shelves.

"Only one more day and then it will be the time to eat. I
didn't take but one bowl of hasty pudding this morning, so I
shall have plenty of room when the nice things come," confided
Seth to Sol, as he cracked a large hazelnut as easily as a squirrel.

"No need of my starvin' beforehand. I always have room
enough, and I'd like to have Thanksgiving every day," answered
Solomon.

"Sakes alive, I don't, boys! It's a marcy it don't come but once
a year. I should be worn to a thread paper[7] with all this extra work
atop of my winter weavin' and spinnin'," laughed their mother,
as she plunged her plump arms into the long bread trough and
began to knead the dough as if a famine were at hand.

Tilly, the oldest girl, a red-cheeked, black-eyed lass[8] of
fourteen, was grinding briskly at the mortar, for spices were
costly, and not a grain must be wasted. Prue kept time with the
chopper, and the twins sliced away at the apples till their little
brown arms ached, for all knew how to work, and did so now
with a will.

"I think it's real fun to have Thanksgiving at home. I'm sorry
Gran'ma is sick, so we can't go there as usual, but I like to mess
'round here, don't you, girls?" asked Tilly, pausing to take a **sniff**
at the spicy pestle.

5 *literary*: happy and not worried about anything
6 *old-fashioned*: 'a sight of victuals' means a lot of food
7 *old-fashioned*: worn out, completely tired
8 *informal*: a girl, or a young woman

"It will be kind of lonesome with only our own folks."

"I like to see all the cousins and aunts, and have games, and sing," cried the twins, who were regular little romps[9], and could run, swim, coast, and shout as well as their brothers.

"I don't care a **mite** for all that. It will be so nice to eat dinner together, warm and comfortable at home," said quiet Prue, who loved her own cozy **nooks** like a cat.

"Come, girls, fly 'round and get your chores done, so we can clear away for dinner jest as soon as I clap my bread into the oven," called Mrs. Bassett presently, as she rounded off the last loaf of brown bread which was to feed the hungry mouths that seldom tasted any other.

"Here's a man comin' up the hill lively!" "Guess it's Gad Hopkins. Pa told him to bring a dezzen oranges, if they warn't too high[10]!" shouted Sol and Seth, running to the door, while the girls smacked their lips at the thought of this rare treat, and Baby threw his apple overboard[11], as if getting ready for a new cargo.

But all were doomed to disappointment, for it was not Gad, with the much-desired fruit. It was a stranger, who threw himself off his horse and hurried up to Mr. Bassett in the yard, with some brief message that made the farmer drop his ax and look so sober that his wife guessed at once some bad news had come; and crying, "Mother's wuss! I know she is!" Out ran the good woman, forgetful of the flour on her arms and the oven waiting for its most important **batch**.

The man said old Mr. Chadwick, down to Keene, stopped him as he passed, and told him to tell Mrs. Bassett her mother was failin' fast, and she'd better come today. He knew no more, and having delivered his **errand** he rode away, saying it looked like snow and he must be jogging, or he wouldn't get home till night.

---

9 (normally a verb) if children romp, they play or move around in a lively and often noisy way

10 if the price wasn't too high

11 *figurative*: off a boat or ship and into the water, here means he threw it out of his cradle

"We must go right off, Eldad. Hitch up[12], and I'll be ready in less'n no time," said Mrs. Bassett, wasting not a minute in tears and lamentations, but pulling off her apron as she went in, with her head in a sad **jumble** of bread, anxiety, turkey, sorrow, haste, and cider applesauce.

A few words told the story, and the children left their work to help her get ready, mingling their grief for "Gran'ma" with regrets for the lost dinner.

"I'm dreadful sorry, dears, but it can't be helped. I couldn't cook nor eat no way now, and if that blessed woman gets better sudden, as she has before, we'll have cause for thanksgivin', and I'll give you a dinner you won't forget in a hurry," said Mrs. Bassett, as she tied on her brown silk pumpkin-hood[13], with a **sob** for the good old mother who had made it for her.

Not a child complained after that, but ran about helpfully, bringing moccasins[14], heating the footstone[15], and getting ready for a long drive, because Gran'ma lived twenty miles away, and there were no railroads in those parts to whisk people to and fro like magic. By the time the old yellow **sleigh** was at the door, the bread was in the oven, and Mrs. Bassett was waiting, with her camlet **cloak** on, and the baby done up like a small bale of blankets.

"Now, Eph, you must look after the cattle like a man and keep up the fires, for there's a storm brewin', and neither the children nor dumb critters must suffer," said Mr. Bassett, as he turned up the collar of his rough coat and put on his blue **mittens**, while the old **mare** shook her bells as if she preferred a trip to Keene to hauling wood all day.

"Tilly, put extry comfortables[16] on the beds to-night, the wind is so searchin' up chamber[17]. Have the baked beans and Injun-puddin'[18] for dinner, and whatever you do, don't let the boys get

12 fasten a horse to something such as a post or wagon
13 a hat that ties under your chin
14 soft leather shoes with a flat heel
15 a metal box filled with hot coals used to keep travellers' feet warm on cold journeys
16 US English: (normally *comforter*) a warm cover for your bed
17 the cold wind gets into the bedroom
18 a traditional American dessert

at the mince-pies, or you'll have them down sick. I shall come back the minute I can leave Mother. Pa will come to-morrer anyway, so keep **snug** and be good. I depend on you, my darter; use your jedgment, and don't let nothin' happen while Mother's away."

"Yes'm, yes'm – good-bye, good-bye!" called the children, as Mrs. Bassett was packed into the sleigh and driven away, leaving a stream of directions behind her.

Eph, the sixteen-year-old boy, immediately put on his biggest boots, assumed a sober, responsible manner and surveyed his little responsibilities with a paternal **air**, drolly[19] like his father's. Tilly tied on her mother's bunch of keys, rolled up the sleeves of her homespun gown, and began to order about the younger girls. They soon forgot poor Granny, and found it great fun to keep house all alone, for Mother seldom left home, but ruled her family in the good old-fashioned way. There were no servants, for the little daughters were Mrs. Bassett's only maids, and the stout boys helped their father, all working happily together with no wages but love; learning in the best manner the use of the heads and hands with which they were to make their own way in the world.

The few flakes that caused the farmer to predict bad weather soon increased to a regular snowstorm, with gusts of wind, for up among the hills winter came early and **lingered** long. But the children were busy, gay, and warm indoors, and never minded the rising gale nor the whirling white storm outside.

Tilly got them a good dinner, and when it was over the two elder girls went to their spinning, for in the kitchen stood the big and little wheels, and baskets of wool rolls ready to be twisted into yarn for the winter's knitting, and each day brought its **stint** of work to the daughters, who hoped to be as thrifty as their mother.

Eph kept up a glorious fire, and superintended the small boys, who popped corn and whittled boats on the hearth; while Roxy and Rhody dressed corncob dolls[20] in the settle corner, and

19 *unusual*: from the adjective *droll*, in a funny way
20 traditional homemade dolls

Bose, the brindled **mastiff**, lay on the braided mat, luxuriously warming his old legs. Thus employed, they made a pretty picture, these rosy boys and girls, in their homespun suits, with the rustic toys or tasks which most children nowadays would find very poor or tiresome.

Tilly and Prue sang, as they stepped to and fro, drawing out the smoothly twisted threads to the musical hum of the great spinning wheels. The little girls chattered like magpies[21] over their dolls and the new bedspread they were planning to make, all white dimity stars on a blue calico ground, as a Christmas present to Ma. The boys roared at Eph's jokes, and had **rough and tumble** games over Bose, who didn't mind them in the least; and so the afternoon wore pleasantly away.

At sunset the boys went out to feed the cattle, bring in heaps of wood, and lock up for the night, as the lonely farmhouse seldom had visitors after dark. The girls got the simple supper of brown bread and milk, baked apples, and a doughnut all 'round as a treat. Then they sat before[22] the fire, the sisters knitting, the brothers with books or games, for Eph loved reading, and Sol and Seth never failed to play a few games of Morris with barley corns, on the little board they had themselves at one corner of the dresser.

"Read out a piece," said Tilly from Mother's chair, where she sat in state[23], finishing off the sixth woolen sock she had knit that month.

"It's the old history book, but here's a bit you may like, since it's about our folks," answered Eph, turning the yellow page to look at a picture of two quaintly dressed children in some ancient castle.

"Yes, read that. I always like to hear about the Lady Matildy I was named for, and Lord Bassett, Pa's great-great-great grandpa. He's only a farmer now, but it's nice to know we were somebody two or three hundred years ago," said Tilly, bridling[24] and tossing her curly head as she fancied the Lady Matilda might have done.

21 a noisy black and white bird with a long tail
22 *formal*: in front of
23 if an important person sits in state, the public are formally allowed to visit
24 throw up your head and draw in your chin like a horse

"Don't read the queer[25] words, 'cause we don't understand 'em. Tell it," commanded Roxy, from the cradle, where she was drowsily cuddled with Rhody.

"Well, a long time ago, when Charles the First was in prison, Lord Bassett was a true friend to him," began Eph, plunging into his story without delay. "The lord had some papers that would have **hung** a lot of people if the king's enemies got hold of 'em, so when he heard one day, all of a sudden, that soldiers were at the castle gate to carry him off, he had just time to call his girl to him and say: 'I may be going to my death, but I won't betray my master. There is no time to burn the papers, and I cannot take them with me; they are hidden in the old leathern chair where I sit. No one knows this but you, and you must guard them till I come or send you a safe messenger to take them away. Promise me to be brave and silent, and I can go without fear.' You see, he wasn't afraid to die, but he was to seem a traitor. Lady Matildy promised solemnly, and the words were hardly out of her mouth when the men came in, and her father was carried away a prisoner and sent off to the Tower[26]."

"But she didn't cry; she just called her brother, and sat down in that chair, with her head leaning back on those papers, like a queen, and waited while the soldiers hunted the house over for 'em: wasn't that a smart girl?" cried Tilly, **beaming** with pride, for she was named for this ancestress, and knew the story by heart.

"I reckon she was scared, though, when the men came swearin' in and asked her if she knew anything about it. The boy did his part then, for he didn't know, and fired up and stood before his sister; and he says, says he, as bold as a lion: 'If my lord had told us where the papers be, we would die before we would betray him. But we are children and know nothing, and it is cowardly of you to try to fight us with oaths and drawn swords!'"

As Eph quoted from the book, Seth planted himself before Tilly, with the long **poker** in his hand, saying, as he flourished it valiantly[27]:

25 *old-fashioned*: strange
26 The Tower of London was used as a prison in the 17th century, the time of the story
27 *literary*: in a very brave and determined way, especially in a difficult situation

"Why didn't the boy take his father's sword and lay about[28] him? I would, if any one was ha'sh to Tilly."

"You bantam[29]! He was only a bit of a boy, and couldn't do anything. Sit down and hear the rest of it," commanded Tilly, with a pat on the yellow head, and a private resolve that Seth should have the largest piece of pie at dinner next day, as reward for his **chivalry**.

"Well, the men went off after turning the castle out of the window[30], but they said they should come again; so faithful Matildy was full of trouble, and hardly dared to leave the room where the chair stood. All day she sat there, and at night her sleep was so full of fear about it, that she often got up and went to see that all was safe. The servants thought the fright had hurt her **wits**, and let her be, but Rupert, the boy, stood by her and never was afraid of her queer ways. She was 'a **pious** maid,' the book says, and often spent the long evenings reading the Bible, with her brother by her, all alone in the great room, with no one to help her bear her secret, and no good news of her father. At last, word came that the king was dead and his friends **banished** out of England. Then the poor children were in a sad plight[31], for they had no mother, and the servants all ran away, leaving only one faithful old man to help them."

"But the father did come?" cried Roxy, eagerly.

"You'll see," continued Eph, half telling, half reading. "Matilda was sure he would, so she sat on in the big chair, guarding the papers, and no one could get her away, till one day a man came with her father's ring and told her to give up the secret. She knew the ring, but would not tell until she had asked many questions, so as to be very sure, and while the man answered all about her father and the king, she looked at him sharply. Then she stood up and said, in a **tremble**, for there was something strange about the man: 'Sir, I doubt you in spite of the ring, and I will not answer till you pull off the false beard you

28 *old-fashioned*: attack someone by hitting them
29 a type of small chicken, used here as an insult
30 if you turn something out, you remove everything from it
31 *literary*: a sad, serious or difficult situation

wear, that I may see your face and know if you are my father's friend or foe.' Off came the disguise, and Matilda found it was my lord himself, come to take them with him out of England. He was very proud of that faithful girl, I guess, for the old chair still stands in the castle, and the name keeps in the family, Pa says, even over here, where some of the Bassetts came along with the Pilgrims."

"Our Tilly would have been as brave, I know, and she looks like the old picter down to Gran'ma's[32], don't she, Eph?" cried Prue, who admired her bold, bright sister very much.

"Well, I think you'd do the settin' part best, Prue, you are so patient. Till would fight like a wild cat, but she can't hold her tongue[33] worth a cent" answered Eph; whereat[34] Tilly pulled his hair, and the story ended with a general frolic.

When the moon-faced clock behind the door struck nine, Tilly tucked up the children under the "extry comfortables," and having kissed them all around, as Mother did, crept into her own nest, never minding the little drifts of snow that sifted in upon her coverlet between the **shingles** of the roof, nor the storm that raged without[35].

As if he felt the need of unusual vigilance, old Bose lay down on the mat before the door, and pussy had the warm hearth all to herself. If any late wanderer had looked in at midnight, he would have seen the fire blazing up again, and in the cheerful glow the old cat blinking her yellow eyes, as she sat bolt upright beside the spinning wheel, like some sort of household **goblin**, guarding the children while they slept.

When they woke, like early birds, it still snowed, but up the little Bassetts jumped, broke the ice in their jugs, and went down with cheeks glowing like winter apples, after a brisk **scrub** and scramble into their clothes. Eph was off to the barn, and Tilly soon had a great kettle of mush[36] ready, which, with milk

32 the picture at Grandma's house (non standard use of preposition *to*)
33 say nothing, although you want to speak
34 *very formal*: an old word meaning 'as a result of the action that has been mentioned'
35 *old-fashioned*: outside
36 *US English*: a thick food made by boiling maize flour with water or milk, eaten at breakfast

warm from the cows made a wholesome breakfast for the seven hearty children.

"Now about dinner," said the young housekeeper, as the pewter[37] spoons stopped clattering, and the **earthen** bowls stood empty.

"Ma said, have what we liked, but she didn't expect us to have a real Thanksgiving dinner, because she won't be here to cook it, and we don't know how," began Prue, doubtfully.

"I can roast a turkey and make a pudding as well as anybody, I guess. The pies are all ready, and if we can't boil vegetables and so on, we don't deserve any dinner," cried Tilly, **burning** to distinguish herself, and bound to enjoy to the utmost her brief authority.

"Yes, yes!" cried all the boys, "let's have a dinner anyway; Ma won't care, and the good victuals will spoil if they ain't eaten right up."

"Pa is coming tonight, so we won't have dinner till late; that will be real **genteel** and give us plenty of time," added Tilly, suddenly realizing the novelty of the task she had undertaken.

"Did you ever roast a turkey?" asked Roxy, with an air of deep interest.

"Should you darst to try?" said Rhody, in an **awe-stricken** tone.

"You will see what I can do. Ma said I was to use my judgment about things, and I'm going to. All you children have got to do is to keep out of the way, and let Prue and me work. Eph, I wish you'd put a fire in the best room, so the little ones can play in there. We shall want the settin-room for the table, and I won't have them pickin' round[38] when we get things fixed," commanded Tilly, bound to make her short **reign** a brilliant one.

"I don't know about that. Ma didn't tell us to," began cautious Eph who felt that this invasion of the sacred[39] best parlor was a daring step.

37 a grey metal used in the past for making plates, cups, and other objects
38 *unusual*: getting in someone's way
39 *figurative*: here used to mean important and worthy of respect; normally, considered holy or connected with a god or gods

"Don't we always do it Sundays and Thanksgivings? Wouldn't Ma wish the children kept safe and warm anyhow? Can I get up a nice dinner with four **rascals** under my feet all the time? Come, now, if you want roast turkey and onions, plum-puddin' and mince-pie, you'll have to do as I tell you, and be lively about it."

Tilly spoke with such spirit, and her suggestion was so irresistible, that Eph gave in, and, laughing good-naturedly, tramped away to heat up the best room, devoutly hoping that nothing serious would happen to punish such **audacity**.

The young folks delightedly trooped away to destroy the order of that prim apartment with housekeeping under the black horsehair sofa, "horseback-riders" on the arms of the best rocking chair, and an Indian war dance all over the well-waxed furniture. Eph, finding the society of peaceful sheep and cows more to his mind than that of two excited sisters, lingered over his chores in the barn as long as possible, and left the girls in peace.

Now Tilly and Prue were in their glory[40], and as soon as the breakfast things were out of the way, they prepared for a grand cooking time. They were handy girls, though they had never heard of a cooking school, never touched a piano, and knew nothing of embroidery beyond the samplers which hung framed in the parlor; one ornamented with a pink mourner under a blue weeping willow, the other with this pleasing verse, each word being done in a different color, which gave the effect of a distracted rainbow:

This sampler neat was worked by me,
In my twelfth year, Prudence B.

Both rolled up their sleeves, put on their largest aprons, and got out all the spoons, dishes, pots, and pans they could find, "so as to have everything handy," Prue said.

"Now, sister, we'll have dinner at five; Pa will be here by that time, if he is coming tonight, and be so surprised to find us all

40 feel very happy and comfortable in a situation (normally, 'be in your element')

ready, for he won't have had any very nice victuals if Gran'ma is so sick," said Tilly, importantly. "I shall give the children a piece at noon" (Tilly meant luncheon[41]); "doughnuts and cheese, with apple pie and cider, will please 'em. There's beans for Eph; he likes it cold, so we won't stop to warm it up, for there's lots to do, and I don't mind saying to you I'm dreadful dubersome about the turkey."

"It's all ready but the stuffing, and roasting is as easy as can be. I can baste first-rate. Ma always likes to have me, I'm so patient and stiddy, she says," answered Prue, for the responsibility of this great **undertaking** did not rest upon her, so she took a cheerful view of things.

"I know, but it's the stuffin' that troubles me," said Tilly, rubbing her round elbows as she eyed the immense **fowl** laid out on a platter before her. "I don't know how much I want, nor what sort of yarbs to put in, and he's so awful big, I'm kind of afraid of him."

"I ain't! I fed him all summer, and he never gobbled[42] at me. I feel real mean to be thinking of gobbling him, poor old chap," laughed Prue, patting her departed pet with an air of mingled affection and appetite.

"Well, I'll get the puddin' off my mind fust, for it ought to bile all day. Put the big kettle on, and see that the spit is clean, while I get ready."

Prue obediently tugged away at the crane, with its black hooks, from which hung the iron teakettle and three-legged pot; then she settled the long spit in the grooves made for it in the tall andirons, and put the dripping pan underneath, for in those days meat was roasted as it should be, not baked in ovens.

Meantime Tilly attacked the plum pudding. She felt pretty sure of coming out right, here, for she had seen her mother do it so many times, it looked very easy. So in went suet and fruit; all sorts of spice, to be sure she got the right ones, and brandy instead of wine. But she forgot both sugar and salt, and tied it

41 *old-fashioned*: lunch
42 gobble has two meanings: 1) eat something quickly and often noisily, and 2) make the sound made by a turkey. Prue uses both meanings to make a joke.

in the cloth so tightly that it had no room to **swell**, so it would come out as heavy as lead and as hard as a cannonball, if the bag did not burst and spoil it all. Happily unconscious of these mistakes, Tilly popped it into the pot, and proudly watched it **bobbing** about before she put the cover on and left it to its fate.

"I can't remember what flavorin' Ma puts in," she said, when she had got her bread well soaked for stuffing. "Sage and onions and applesauce go with goose, but I can't feel sure of anything but pepper and salt for a turkey."

"Ma puts in some kind of mint, I know, but I forget whether it is spearmint, peppermint, or pennyroyal," answered Prue, in a tone of doubt, but trying to show her knowledge of "yarbs," or, at least, of their names.

"Seems to me it's sweet marjoram or summer savory. I guess we'll put both in, and then we are sure to be right. The best is up garret; you run and get some, while I mash the bread," commanded Tilly, diving into the mess.

Away trotted Prue, but in her haste she got catnip[43] and wormwood[44], for the garret was darkish, and Prue's little nose was so full of the smell of the onions she had been peeling, that everything smelt of them. Eager to be of use, she pounded up the herbs and scattered the mixture with a liberal hand into the bowl.

"It doesn't smell just right, but I suppose it will when it is cooked," said Tilly, as she filled the empty stomach, that seemed aching for food, and sewed it up with the blue yarn, which happened to be handy. She forgot to tie down his legs and wings, but she set him by till his hour came, well satisfied with her work.

It took a long time to get all the vegetables ready, for, as the cellar was full, the girls thought they would have every sort. Eph helped, and by noon all was ready for cooking, and the cranberry sauce, a good deal **scorched**, was cooking in the lean-to[45].

43 a plant with a strong smell that attracts cats and makes them excited
44 a bitter plant used in some medicines and alcoholic drinks
45 part of the hearth

Luncheon was a lively meal, and doughnuts and cheese vanished in such quantities that Tilly feared no one would have an appetite for her **sumptuous** dinner. The boys assured her they would be starving by five o'clock.

"Now you all go and coast, while Prue and I set the table and get out the best chiny," said Tilly, **bent on** having her dinner look well, no matter what its other failings might be.

Out came the rough **sleds**, on went the round hoods, old hats, red cloaks, and moccasins, and away trudged the four younger Bassetts, to disport[46] themselves in the snow, and try the ice down by the old mill, where the great wheel turned and splashed so merrily in the summertime.

Eph took his fiddle[47] and scraped away to his heart's content in the parlor, while the girls, after a short rest, set the table and made all ready to dish up the dinner when that exciting moment came. It was not at all the sort of table we see now, but would look very plain and countrified to us, with its green-handled knives, and two-pronged steel forks, its red-and-white china, and pewter platters, **scoured** till they shone, with mugs and spoons to match, and a brown jug for the cider. The cloth was coarse, but white as snow, and the little maids had seen the blue-eyed flax[48] grow, out of which their mother wove the linen; they had watched and watched while it bleached in the green meadow. They had no napkins and little silver; but the best tankard[49] and Ma's few wedding spoons were set forth in state. Nuts and apples at the corners gave an air, and the place of honor was left in the middle for the oranges yet to come.

"Don't it look beautiful?" said Prue, when they paused to admire the general effect.

"Pretty nice, I think. I wish Ma could see how well we can do it," began Tilly, when a loud **howling** startled both girls, and sent them flying to the window. The short afternoon had passed so quickly that twilight had come before they knew it, and now,

46 *old-fashioned*: enjoy yourself
47 a violin
48 a plant with small blue flowers that is grown for the fibres in its stem and the oil in its seeds
49 a large metal or glass cup for drinking with a handle and sometimes with a lid

as they looked out through the gathering dusk, they saw four small black figures tearing up the road, to come bursting in, all screaming at once: "The bear, the bear! Eph, get the gun! He's coming, he's coming!"

Eph had dropped his fiddle, and got down his gun before the girls could calm the children enough to tell their story, which they did in a somewhat incoherent manner. "Down in the holler, coastin', we heard a growl," began Sol, with his eyes as big as saucers. "I see him fust lookin' over the wall," roared Seth, eager to get his share of honor.

"Awful big and **shaggy**," **quavered** Roxy, clinging to Tilly, while Rhody hid in Prue's skirts, and piped out:

"His great paws kept clawing at us, and I was so scared my legs would hardly go."

"We ran away as fast as we could go, and he came growlin' after us. He's awful hungry, and he'll eat every one of us if he gets in," continued Sol, looking about him for a safe retreat.

"Oh, Eph, don't let him eat us," cried both little girls, flying upstairs to hide under their mother's bed, as their surest shelter.

"No danger of that, you little geese. I'll shoot him as soon as he comes. Get out of the way, boys," and Eph raised the window to get good aim.

"There he is! Fire away, and don't miss!" cried Seth, hastily following Sol, who had climbed to the top of the dresser as a good perch from which to view the approaching **fray**.

Prue retired to the hearth as if bent on dying at her post rather than desert the turkey, now "browning beautiful," as she expressed it. But Tilly boldly stood at the open window, ready to lend a hand if the enemy proved too much for Eph.

All had seen bears, but none had ever come so near before, and even brave Eph felt that the big brown beast slowly trotting up the dooryard was an unusually **formidable** specimen. He was growling horribly, and stopped now and then as if to rest and shake himself.

"Get the ax, Tilly, and if I should miss, stand ready to keep him off while I load again," said Eph, anxious to kill his first bear in style and alone; a girl's help didn't count.

Tilly flew for the ax, and was at her brother's side by the time the bear was near enough to be dangerous. He stood on his hind legs, and seemed to sniff with relish the savory odors that poured out of the window.

"Fire, Eph!" cried Tilly, firmly.

"Wait till he **rears** again. I'll get a better shot then" answered the boy, while Prue covered her ears to shut out the bang, and the small boys cheered from their dusty refuge among the pumpkins.

But a very singular thing happened next, and all who saw it stood amazed, for suddenly Tilly threw down the ax, flung open the door, and ran straight into the arms of the bear, who stood erect to receive her, while his growlings changed to a loud "Haw, haw!" that startled the children more than the report of a gun.

"It's Gad Hopkins, tryin' to fool us!" cried Eph, much disgusted at the loss of his prey, for these hardy boys loved to hunt and prided themselves on the number of wild animals and birds they could shoot in a year.

"Oh, Gad, how could you scare us so?" laughed Tilly, still held fast in one shaggy arm of the bear, while the other drew a dozen oranges from some deep pocket in the buffalo-skin coat, and fired them into the kitchen with such good aim that Eph ducked, Prue screamed, and Sol and Seth came down much quicker than they went up.

"Wal, you see I got upsot[50] over yonder, and the old horse went home while I was **floundering** in a drift, so I tied on the buffalers to tote[51] 'em easy, and come along till I see the children playin' in the holler. I jest meant to give 'em a little scare, but they run like partridges, and I kep' up the joke to see how Eph would like this sort of company," and Gad haw-hawed[52] again.

"You'd have had a warm welcome if we hadn't found you out. I'd have put a bullet through you **in a jiffy**, old chap," said Eph, coming out to shake hands with the young giant, who was only a year or two older than himself.

50 his cart was upset, it fell over
51 *unusual*: carry or pull
52 *unusual*: laughed

"Come in and set up to dinner with us. Prue and I have done it all ourselves, and Pa will be along soon, I reckon," cried Tilly, trying to escape.

"Couldn't, no ways. My folks will think I'm dead ef I don't get along home, sence the horse and sleigh have gone ahead empty I've done my arrant[53] and had my joke; now I want my pay, Tilly," and Gad took a hearty kiss from the rosy cheeks of his "little sweetheart," as he called her. His own cheeks tingled with the smart **slap** she gave him as she ran away, calling out that she hated bears and would bring her ax next time.

"I ain't afeared – your sharp eyes found me out: and ef you run into a bear's arms you must expect a hug," answered Gad, as he pushed back the robe and settled his fur cap more becomingly[54].

"I should have known you in a minute if I hadn't been asleep when the girls squalled[55]. You did it well, though, and I advise you not to try it again in a hurry, or you'll get shot," said Eph, as they parted, he rather **crestfallen** and Gad in high glee.

"My sakes alive – the turkey is all burnt one side, and the kettles have biled over so the pies I put to warm are all ashes!" scolded Tilly, as the flurry subsided and she remembered her dinner.

"Well, I can't help it. I couldn't think of victuals when I expected to be eaten alive myself, could I?" pleaded poor Prue, who had **tumbled** into the cradle when the rain of oranges began.

Tilly laughed, and all the rest joined in, so good humor was restored, and the spirits of the younger ones were revived by sucks from the one orange which passed from hand to hand with great rapidity while the older girls dished up the dinner. They were just struggling to get the pudding out of the cloth when Roxy called out: "Here's Pa!"

"There's folks with him," added Rhody.

"Lots of 'em! I see two big sleighs chock full," shouted Seth, peering through the dusk.

53 errand
54 *old-fashioned*: in a way that makes you look attractive
55 cry loudly

"It looks like a seminary. Guess Gran'ma's dead and come up to be buried here," said Sol, in a solemn tone. This startling suggestion made Tilly, Prue, and Eph hasten to look out, full of dismay at such an ending of their festival.

"If that is a funeral, the mourners are uncommonly jolly," said Eph, dryly, as merry voices and loud laughter broke the white silence without.

"I see Aunt Cinthy, and Cousin Hetty – and there's Mose and Amos. I do declare, Pa's bringin' 'em all home to have some fun here," cried Prue, as she recognized one familiar face after another.

"Oh, my patience! Ain't I glad I got dinner, and don't I hope it will turn out good!" exclaimed Tilly, while the twins pranced with delight, and the small boys roared:

"Hooray for Pa! Hooray for Thanksgivin'!"

The cheer was answered heartily, and in came Father, Mother, Baby, aunts, and cousins, all in great spirits; and all much surprised to find such a festive welcome awaiting them.

"Ain't Gran'ma dead at all?" asked Sol, in the midst of the kissing and handshaking.

"Bless your heart, no! It was all a mistake of old Mr. Chadwick's. He's as deaf as an adder[56], and when Mrs. Brooks told him Mother was mendin' fast, and she wanted me to come down today, certain sure, he got the message all wrong, and give it to the fust person passin' in such a way as to scare me 'most to death, and send us down in a hurry. Mother was sittin' up as chirk[57] as you please, and dreadful sorry you didn't all come."

"So, to keep the house quiet for her, and give you a taste of the fun, your Pa fetched us all up to spend the evenin', and we are goin' to have a jolly time on't, to jedge by the looks of things," said Aunt Cinthy, briskly finishing the tale when Mrs. Bassett paused for want of breath.

"What in the world put it into your head we was comm', and set you to gittin' up such a supper?" asked Mr. Bassett, looking about him, well pleased and much surprised at the plentiful table.

56 a harmless snake that lives in North America
57 *old-fashioned US English*: cheerful

Tilly modestly began to tell, but the others **broke in** and sang her praises in a sort of chorus, in which bears, pies, and oranges were oddly mixed. Great satisfaction was expressed by all, and Tilly and Prue were so elated by the commendation of Ma and the aunts, that they set forth their dinner, sure everything was perfect.

But when the eating began, which it did the moment wraps[58] were off; then their pride got a fall[59]; for the first person who tasted the stuffing (it was big Cousin Mose, and that made it harder to bear) nearly choked over the **bitter** morsel[60].

"Tilly Bassett, whatever made you put wormwood and catnip in your stuffin'?" demanded Ma, trying not to be severe, for all the rest were laughing, and Tilly looked ready to cry.

"I did it," said Prue, nobly taking all the blame, which caused Pa to kiss her **on the spot**, and declare that it didn't do a mite of harm, for the turkey was all right.

"I never seen onions cooked better. All the vegetables is well done, and the dinner a credit to you, my dears," declared Aunt Cinthy, with her mouth full of the fragrant vegetable she praised.

The pudding was an **utter** failure in spite of the blazing brandy in which it lay – as hard and heavy as one of the stone balls on Squire Dunkin's great gate. It was speedily whisked out of sight, and all fell upon the pies, which were perfect. But Tilly and Prue were much depressed, and didn't recover their spirits till dinner was over and the evening fun well under way.

"Blind-man's bluff," "Hunt the slipper," "Come, Philander," and other lively games soon set everyone bubbling over with jollity, and when Eph **struck up** "Money Musk" on his fiddle, old and young fell into their places for a dance. All down the long kitchen they stood, Mr. and Mrs. Bassett at the top, the twins at the bottom, and then away they went, heeling and toeing, cutting pigeon-wings[61], and taking their steps in a way

58 *old-fashioned*: outer clothes such as coats and jackets
59 from the saying: 'Pride comes before a fall'. This means: 'If you are too confident you will make mistakes'.
60 *formal*: a small piece of food
61 these are all dance steps for folk dancing

that would convulse[62] modern children with their new-fangled[63] romps called dancing. Mose and Tilly covered themselves with glory by the vigor with which they kept it up, till fat Aunt Cinthy fell into a chair, breathlessly declaring that a very little of such exercise was enough for a woman of her "heft[64]."

Apples and cider, chat and singing, finished the evening, and after a grand kissing all round, the guests drove away in the clear moonlight which came out to cheer their long drive.

When the jingle of the last bell had died away, Mr. Bassett said soberly, as they stood together on the hearth:

"Children, we have special cause to be thankful that the sorrow we expected was changed into joy, so we'll read a chapter 'fore we go to bed, and give thanks where thanks is due."

Then Tilly set out the light stand with the big Bible on it, and a candle on each side, and all sat quietly in the firelight, smiling as they listened with happy hearts to the sweet old words that fit all times and seasons so beautifully.

When the good-nights were over, and the children in bed, Prue put her arm round Tilly and whispered tenderly, for she felt her shake, and was sure she was crying:

"Don't mind about the old stuffin' and puddin', deary – nobody cared, and Ma said we really did do surprisin' well for such young girls."

The laughter Tilly was trying to **smother** broke out then, and was so infectious, Prue could not help joining her, even before she knew the cause of the merriment.

"I was mad about the mistakes, but don't care enough to cry. I'm laughing to think how Gad fooled Eph and I found him out. I thought Mose and Amos would have died over it, when I told them, it was so funny," explained Tilly, when she got her breath.

"I was so scared that when the first orange hit me, I thought it was a bullet, and scrabbled into the cradle as fast as I could.

---

62 if you are convulsed with laughter, your body moves in an uncontrolled way
63 used for describing things that you do not like because they are very modern and complicated
64 weight

It was real mean to frighten the little ones so," laughed Prue, as Tilly gave a growl.

Here a smart **rap** on the wall of the next room caused a sudden **lull** in the fun, and Mrs. Bassett's voice was heard, saying warningly, "Girls, go to sleep immediate, or you'll wake the baby."

"Yes'm," answered two meek voices, and after a few **irrepressible** giggles, silence reigned, broken only by an occasional snore from the boys, or the soft scurry of mice in the buttery, taking their part in this old-fashioned Thanksgiving.

Post-reading activities

Understanding the story

Use these questions to help you check that you have understood the story.

The day before Thanksgiving

1   What can be seen in the house to suggest that the family is preparing for a celebration?
2   What are the girls doing at the beginning of the story? Where are the boys?
3   Why didn't Seth eat much at breakfast?
4   How does Prue's attitude to where they spend Thanksgiving differ from her twin sisters'?
5   How many people travel to Gran'ma's house? How many stay on the farm?
6   What instructions are given before they leave? Who by? Who to?
7   What ways do the children entertain themselves after the midday meal?
8   Why do Tilly and the other children like listening to the story in the old history book?
9   Why does Lord Bassett ask his daughter to hide the papers?
10 Why does Tilly decide to give Seth a large piece of pie?
11 Why does Lord Basset hide his identity from his children at first?
12 What makes Tilly pull her brother's hair and start a play fight?

Thanksgiving Day

13 What does the morning routine consist of?
14 When Tilly decides to make a proper Thanksgiving dinner, why does she ask Eph to make a fire in the parlour? Why is he reluctant to let the younger children in there?
15 Which of the girls is less confident about the cooking? What is she worried about most?
16 What mistakes does Prue make when preparing the plum pudding?
17 What do the others do after lunch while the older girls prepare the table?
18 Who sees the bear first?
19 Why has Gad come to visit them?
20 Why is Eph disappointed that it is Gad?
21 The children are surprised when they see their relatives arrive, but why are the adults surprised?
22 How many people sit down for dinner?

23 What tastes good? What can't they eat? Why?
24 What do they do after supper?
25 What do they do before bed?
26 What does Prue misunderstand about her sister once they are in bed?
27 What are the two girls laughing about at the end of the day?

Language study

Grammar

Uses of *should*

Should has a variety of functions in *An Old-Fashioned Thanksgiving*. First, as in modern everyday English, *should* is used for explaining or asking about the right or sensible thing to do or the right way to behave:

> In those days meat was roasted as it **should** be, not baked in ovens.

A formal, old-fashioned use of *should* is when talking about a situation in the past when you said or knew what you would do or what would happen:

> They said they **should** come again

It is used for saying what someone decides, suggests or orders:

> Sit down and hear the rest of it," commanded Tilly, with a pat on the yellow head, and a private resolve that Seth **should** have the largest piece of pie at dinner next day

These last two functions are examples of reported speech, where *should* acts as the past of *shall*:

> 'We **shall** come again'

> 'Seth **shall** have the largest piece of pie …'

Just as *will* usually replaces *shall* in modern English, *would* replaces *should*. Nowadays we are likely to say:

> They said they **would** come again

> Sit down and hear the rest of it," commanded Tilly, with a pat on the yellow head, and a private resolve that Seth **would** have the largest piece of pie at dinner next day

Would is also the modern replacement in another old-fashioned use of *should*. It is used for saying what you would do or how you would feel in a situation that you imagine:

It's a marcy it don't come but once a year. I **should** be worn to a thread paper with all this extra work atop of my winter weavin' and spinnin'," laughed their mother.

Finally, *should* is used after 'if' for describing a situation that may possibly happen:

"Get the ax, Tilly, and if I **should** miss, stand ready to keep him off while I load again," said Eph

1 **Look at the instances of *should* in the following sentences. Which could not be replaced with *would*?**

1 Parents should spend as much time with their children as possible.
2 I said that I should be happy to co-operate with the investigation.
3 We realized that we should have to pay a large sum to the lawyers.
4 The committee recommended that the chief executive should be dismissed.
5 I should go mad if I had to spend any longer in this place.
6 If there were a problem, I should know exactly what to do.
7 'Will you come to London?' 'I should love to, but I can't leave Emily here on her own.'
8 If anything should happen to me, please give this letter to my wife.

Fronting as a literary device

When we bring an adverb or adverbial phrase to the beginning of a sentence, this is called 'fronting'. When an adverb is fronted (brought to the beginning of the sentence) the subject and verb are often inverted (they change position).

Normal word order:

Farmer Basset lived up among the New Hampshire hills.

Fronting and inversion:

Up among the New Hampshire hills lived Farmer Bassett.

This is common in old-fashioned writing and story-telling such as fairy tales.

2 **Rewrite these sentences using fronting and inversion.**

1 A cheerful fire roared in the great fireplace.
2 Garlands of dried apples hung on the walls.
3 Crook-necked squashes shone up aloft from the beams.
4 Steaming kettles hung on the crane.

Check your answers in the second paragraph of the story (page 25).

Use of *but* for *except* and *instead*

Normally, *but* is used for joining two ideas or statements when the second one is different from the first one, or seems surprising after the first one:

> *They were poor in money, **but** rich in land and love,*

But can also be used after a negative for introducing what is true instead:

> *Not a child complained after that, **but** ran about helpfully. (= They didn't complain; **instead**, they ran about helpfully)*

It is used especially after words such as 'nothing', 'everyone' or 'anything' to mean 'except':

> *"It's all ready **but** the stuffing"*

It can be used in formal or literary English to mean 'only':

> *I took **but** one bowl of hasty pudding this morning. (= I **only** took one bowl)*

In the colloquial English of the story, however, this is used less formally with a negative:

> *I didn't take **but** one bowl of hasty pudding this morning.*

3 Replace *but* in the sentences below with *instead* or *except*.

1 *"I'll be ready in less'n no time," said Mrs. Bassett, wasting not a minute in tears and lamentations, **but** pulling off her apron as she went in.*

2 *The stout boys helped their father, all working happily together with no wages **but** love*

3 *No one knows this **but** you, and you must guard them till I come*

4 *I can't feel sure of anything **but** pepper and salt for a turkey."*

5 *Mother seldom left home, **but** ruled her family in the good old-fashioned way*

4 Complete the second sentence so that it means the same as the first. Use three words including *but*.

1 You're the only person who knows this.
   Nobody .... you.

2 Though she loved him, she knew she couldn't marry him.
   She loved him .... she couldn't marry him.

3 Nobody stayed where they were on the ship, instead going on deck to see the dolphins.
   Not a person on the ship stayed where they were ....
   deck to see the dolphins.

4 I'm the only person who wants you to stay.
   Everyone wants you to ....
5 The only thing you can see is sky and sea.
   Everywhere you look, you can see nothing .... sea.

Vocabulary

Phrasal verbs

Alcott uses phrasal verbs with very physical images to describe the energetic movements and enthusiasm of the family members. Look at these two sentences:

*She **plunged** her plump arms **into** the long bread trough and began to knead the dough as if a famine were at hand.*

*"Well, a long time ago, when Charles the First was in prison, Lord Bassett was a true friend to him," began Eph, **plunging into** his story without delay.*

The verb *plunge into* in the first sentence describes the downward movement of Mrs Bassett's arms as they enter the dough. In the second sentence the action is not the same. Here, *to plunge into* means to suddenly start doing something with energy and enthusiasm. Although it borrows the image of suddenly entering something, there is no physical movement. We can say that *plunge into* in the first sentence has a literal meaning, whereas in the second sentence it has a figurative meaning.

5 **Look at the verbs in bold. They are all used figuratively. Match the verbs (1–8) to their definitions (a–h).**

*The boy did his part then, for he didn't know, and (1) **fired up** and stood before his sister.*

*They saw four small black figures (2) **tearing up** the road, to come (3) **bursting in**, all screaming at once: "The bear, the bear!"*

*Rhody hid in Prue's skirts, and (4) **piped out**: "His great paws kept clawing at us, and I was so scared my legs would hardly go."*

*Tilly modestly began to tell, but the others (5) **broke in** and sang her praises in a sort of chorus.*

*The pudding ... was speedily whisked out of sight, and all (6) **fell upon** the pies, which were perfect.*

*Other lively games soon set everyone (7) **bubbling over** with jollity, and when Eph struck up "Money Musk" on his fiddle, old and young (8) **fell into** their places for a dance.*

a) be very full of something
b) come in quickly and noisily
c) eat hungrily
d) get angry
e) get into the correct position
f) interrupt
g) run quickly
h) start to speak

6 Complete the sentences below with the correct form of a verb from exercise 5.

1 'Er, excuse me,' a small voice .... from the corner of the room, 'but can I say something?'
2 At the sergeant major's call, the soldiers .... a line against the wall.
3 How can we have a conversation if you keep ....?
4 Just at that moment, Clive .... to the office shouting, 'Don't sign the contract!'
5 She couldn't contain her happiness and kept .... with laughter every few seconds.
6 She was so angry that she just .... and shouted at the waiter in front of the whole restaurant.
7 The team were so hungry after the match that they .... the sandwiches and in minutes they had all disappeared.
8 They came .... to their father: 'Can we go to the park? Please!', they pleaded.

7 There are a lot of words in this story that you may not know. Choose five words from the glossary for each of the categories (a–d).

a) that you really needed to understand in order to enjoy the story
b) that you would like to learn to be able to use
c) that you would like to remember to be able to understand in future
d) that you are not so interested in learning

For each category, think about why you chose those words.

Literary analysis

Plot

1 What are the main events in the story?

2 Stories often include events or problems that threaten to destroy the happiness of the characters in some way, followed by a resolution to these problems. What are the threats to the Bassetts' happiness? How serious are they?

3 The story uses a literary device known as 'a story within a story' when Eph tells the children the story about Lady Matildy. What are the main events in Eph's story? How is it similar to or different from the main story?

4 Where does most of the action take place? Imagine that you adapted the story for the theatre. What would the stage look like? Describe it or draw it.

5 Consider how the story might be different if the following things had occurred:

   the message had not been confused by Mr Chadwick
   Gran'ma had really been sick
   it was a bear, not Gad, that approached the house
   Tilly had not recognized Gad Hopkins

6 What is the main message of the story for you?

The role of food in the story

7 Read the beginning of the story again, up to the point where the stranger arrives with the message. How much of the description and story concerns food?

8 Where does the family's food come from? Who is responsible for producing and collecting it? Who is responsible for preparing it?

9 What impression do you get of the family and their farm from the food?

10 How does Tilly feel when she realizes that more people will be eating her Thanksgiving meal? How do her sister and she feel when they realize there are problems with the meal? Why is it so important to them that the meal should be a success?

Character

11 Who are the main characters in the story? Which characters do you have a clearest image of and why?

12 What do the older children do or say that shows how mature they are? What do they do or say to remind us that they are still children?

13 In general, what are the children's main strengths? Do they have any weaknesses?

14 How are Tilly and Prue similar? What differences of personality are there between them?

15 What do you know about Eph? Think about his age, his upbringing, his interests and the way he behaves in the story. Choose three adjectives to describe him.

16 What was his reaction to Gad's trick? What does this tell you about him? How are Eph and Gad different from one another?

17 In what ways are the main characters similar to the son and daughter in the story about Lord Bassett?

18 How does Tilly feel about Lady Matilda? Why?

19 Do you think that Mr and Mrs Bassett were right to leave their children alone for so long? Why/Why not? Would they have been more or less likely to leave the children alone if the story was set today? Why?

20 Which of the characters do you relate to most?

21 Would you like to have grown up in a family like the Bassetts? Why/Why not?

Narration

22 Who tells the story? Is it one of the characters? How would the story have been different if it had been told from the point of view of
a) Tilly?
b) Mrs Bassett?
c) Eph?

23 Which of these effects, if any, did the story have on you? Why?
It made you more interested in Thanksgiving.
It made you cry or laugh.
It made you feel affectionate towards the children.
It made you think about how children should be brought up.
It made you hungry.
It had another effect on you. What?

24 Look at the following extract. Notice the words and expressions in bold. What is the storyteller's attitude to the family's way of life? Do you think it's an objective opinion?

*Mother seldom left home, but ruled her family in **the good old-fashioned way**. There were no servants, for the little daughters were Mrs. Bassett's only maids, and the stout boys helped their father, all **working happily together with no wages but love**; learning **in the best manner** the use of the heads and hands with which they were to make their own way in the world.*

Can you find any other instances where the storyteller comments on the family's lifestyle in this way? What effect does this have on the story?

25 We are often given details that emphasize certain aspects of the Bassetts' lives. In the following extracts, what aspects of their lives are conveyed by the information in bold?
   a) *When they woke, like early birds, it still snowed, but up the little Bassetts jumped, **broke the ice in their jugs**, and went down with cheeks glowing like winter apples*
   b) *"Now about dinner," said the young housekeeper, as the **pewter** spoons stopped clattering, and the **earthen** bowls stood empty.*
   c) *Two small boys sat … picking out the biggest nuts from the goodly store **their own hands had gathered** in October.*

Style

26 Try reading out loud this sentence from near the beginning of the story. What sounds are repeated? How does the sound of the sentence reflect what the sentence is talking about? What other repetition (of sounds or something else) do you notice in the sentence?

To and fro, from table to hearth, bustled buxom Mrs. Bassett, flushed and floury, but busy and blithe as the queen bee of this busy little hive should be.

27 The colloquial speech of her characters is written directly, as it would have been spoken, with its own special accent, vocabulary and grammar. What effect does this have on the story?

28 When Eph reads the story about Lord Bassett (pages 31–33), we are told that the children knew the story well, and that Eph recounted the story 'half telling, half reading' it. Read the following extract. Which part is told? Which part is read? How does the style of the story change?

"I reckon she was scared, though, when the men came swearin' in and asked her if she knew anything about it. The boy did his part then, for he didn't know, and fired up and stood before his sister; and he says, says he, as bold as a lion: 'If my lord had told us where the papers be, we would die before we would betray him. But we are children and know nothing, and it is cowardly of you to try to fight us with oaths and drawn swords!'"

29 In the same way that nature provides the family with all its needs, it also provides a lot of the imagery in the story. Look at this sentence from the opening paragraph. Notice the use of the word *flock*.

They were poor in money, but rich in land and love, for the wide acres of wood, corn, and pasture land fed, warmed, and clothed the **flock** …

A flock is normally a group of birds or sheep, but it is used here as a metaphor to describe the Bassett family. Look at the following extract. What is Mrs Bassett compared with? And her home and kitchen?

Mrs. Bassett, flushed and floury, but busy and blithe as the queen bee of this busy little hive should be.

30 Look at the following images. Who is being compared with what in each case? What does this tell us about the people? What is the overall effect of so many animal comparisons?

  a) *he cracked a large hazelnut* **as easily as a squirrel**
  b) *It will be so nice to eat dinner together, warm and comfortable at home," said quiet Prue, who loved her own cozy nooks* **like a cat**
  c) *The little girls* **chattered like magpies**
  d) *he says, says he,* **as bold as a lion**: *'If my lord had told us where the papers be, we would die before we would betray him.*
  e) *Till would fight* **like a wild cat**
  f) *When they woke,* **like early birds**, *it still snowed*
  g) *the little Bassetts went down with cheeks glowing like* **winter apples**
  h) *It was all a mistake of old Mr. Chadwick's. He's* **as deaf as an adder**

31 Read the last part of the story, once the guests have gone home.
    How is the Bassett family feeling? How would you describe the
    atmosphere of this final scene? How does this reflect on the story as
    a whole?

*Guidance to the above literary terms, answer keys to all the exercises and
activities, plus a wealth of other reading-practice material, can be found at:
www.macmillanenglish.com/readers.*

The Little Pies

by Alphonse Daudet

About the author

Alphonse Daudet was a nineteenth-century French novelist and short-story writer who first became famous for his descriptions of rural life in southern France. His stories include serious themes concerning French society, set in the countryside and the city. His novels are sentimental in nature, making his readers experience sadness and sympathy for the characters.

Daudet was born in Nîmes, in a region of southern France called Provence, in 1840. His father was a silk merchant, a person who bought and sold expensive fabric. He experienced financial difficulties and the family moved to Lyon, a large city in the east of France, when Alphonse was nine years old. Alphonse was not happy at school but he loved writing, completing a novel when he was just fourteen years old. By 1857, the Daudets had nothing left and the family could no longer support itself. Alphonse was sent to be a teacher in Alès but he hated teaching. His first novel, *La Petite Chose* (*Little Good-For-Nothing*, 1868) is autobiographical and talks about this unhappy time. Fortunately, Alphonse's older brother invited him to come and live with him in Paris. There, he began his professional writing career.

Very soon he had published a collection of love poems and some plays, and was writing articles for newspapers. He began to be recognized as a writer with much promise. The Duke of Morny, an important politician and half-brother of the French Emperor, Napoleon III, gave him a job as one of his secretaries, and this comfortable job gave him the time and financial support to write more freely.

He wrote many short stories between 1865 and 1869, which were regularly published in newspapers. Many were written as letters from the point of view of a Parisian who moves to the Provençal countryside in the south of France to live in a windmill. These were collected and published together in 1869 under the title of *Lettres de mon Moulin* (*Letters from my Windmill*). These light-hearted tales of country life are still read and loved by French people today and are his most famous work. Some of the stories have been made into films.

He was recognized as a serious writer in French literary circles for his later novels, which record many social problems of the time. He was part of the literary movement known as Naturalism. This movement originated in France with the work of Émile Zola and together with two brothers, the Goncourts, they focused on descriptions of the everyday reality of life for ordinary people. He also wrote stories about war. In 1870 he joined the army when France was at war with Prussia (a kingdom in what is now Germany). He was in Paris during the Paris Commune of 1871 (see Background Information below for more details) but escaped the terrible events that occurred afterwards.

He died suddenly in 1897 of a nervous disease that had troubled him for many years. His many novels and short stories are seen as important works, not only in France, but also internationally, and he still stands as one of the most respected writers of his time.

About the story

The Little Pies (in French, *Les Petits Pâtés*) was first published in French in 1873 in a collection of short stories by Daudet titled *Contes du Lundi*. It wasn't printed in English until 1900, when it was translated as *The Monday Tales*. The stories describe French life and larger political events through the lives of ordinary people.

Background information

Food in the story

The pies of the title are a translation of *pâté*, a French word that refers to two different foods: either a soft food made from meat, fish or vegetables that you can spread on bread, or a type of meat pie popular in France. In English, which has many French words to describe food, the word *pâté* (pronounced /ˈpæteɪ/) refers to the first food, the spread.

The little pies in the title are probably *pâtés de Nîmes* fom Daudet's home town. He was so keen on these little pies that he had his butcher from Nîmes deliver them to him in Paris. They are made of pastry, a food made by mixing flour, fat and water, which is then rolled flat, shaped and filled with meat. Although there aren't many ingredients in these pies, they are small individual portions and quite complicated to make. Because of this, these speciality dishes are often bought from bakeries rather than made at home. Prepared food like this would have been expensive: only affordable to wealthier families in the nineteenth century, and something eaten on Sundays and special occasions.

Class in nineteenth century France

Society in Paris and the rest of France was strictly divided into classes, as it was throughout Europe. The upper and middle classes were referred to as the *bourgeoisie*, a term which is used in English to describe the middle classes only. In modern English it expresses disapproval, especially when the middle classes are thought of as being too interested in money and possessions and in being socially respected. In its original meaning, the bourgeoisie were the people who owned land, shops, factories and so on, all the places where things were produced and money created. The bourgeoisie is contrasted with the lower, or working, classes. These were people who did not own the means of making money. Instead they worked for the members of the higher classes. The working class was divided into skilled and unskilled workers. To become skilled in a trade such as cooking, boys as young as ten would work as apprentices for a particular person or company, usually for very low pay, in order to learn the job.

The Paris Commune

The story takes place during the spring of 1871, a time of extreme political instability in Paris. France had recently lost a war with Prussia and there was a lot of anger among the citizens of Paris, especially the workers, who had also been unhappy for a long time about their working and living conditions during the industrial revolution.

The conservative national government, based outside Paris in Versailles, was afraid of the revolutionary political climate in the city. It refused to let Paris govern itself with a city council, something other cities in France could do. However, Paris had significant military power in the form of the National Guard. This was a group of ordinary citizens who were trained as soldiers to keep order and defend Paris from the invading Prussians. The soldiers were known as confederates. The National Guard leaders were suspicious of the government, so they formed their own city council and, when the government tried to take their cannons (large guns that shot metal balls), they hid them and blocked the streets with barricades, temporary structures built across the streets, in order to prevent the government's soldiers from entering the city. The Paris council, or 'Commune', was now in charge of the capital. The French government had lost control.

However, this only lasted a few weeks. The *Versaillais*, or government soldiers, broke through the city's defences on 21st May and took back the city in an aggressive attack. The last days of May became known as 'The Bloody Week'; hundreds of prisoners were taken, National Guardsmen and other people suspected of fighting against the government were executed. Others, like Daudet, managed to escape.

Summary

It may help you to know something about what happens in the story before you read it. Don't worry, this summary does not tell you how the story ends!

Paris is under the control of the socialist Paris Commune, but not for much longer. Conservative government forces are finally breaking the defences and soldiers from Versailles are moving into the capital. All around the city, National Guard soldiers are reinforcing the barricades across the streets and firing their cannons towards the attacking army.

For many Parisians, however, life goes on as normal. A pastry cook, Sureau, has prepared some pies for the Bonnicar family, a wealthy family who live locally, just as he does every Sunday. He orders his young apprentice to take them to their house a few streets away. The apprentice makes his way through the busy streets, determined to get to the house without dropping the pies and so collect his money. Unfortunately, he is distracted by some soldiers marching past and decides to follow them for a while, forgetting that he has to deliver the pies at midday.

Meanwhile, the Bonnicars are getting hungry and impatient. Monsieur Bonnicar, angry with Sureau, decides to go out to look for his pies despite warnings from neighbours that it is not safe on the streets. It is not long before he is stopped and questioned by some soldiers, who are suspicious. His clothes make them think he is a reactionary, someone opposed to any social or political change, and they think he may be a spy. He tries to explain that he is innocent, but they take him away. The course of Monsieur Bonnicar's day changes again when the soldiers are themselves captured, this time by government soldiers, who have entered the city. He and the soldiers are marched away to Versailles.

But what has happened to the apprentice and the little pies?

Pre-reading activities

Key vocabulary

This section will help you familiarize yourself with some of the more specific vocabulary used in the story. You may want to use it to help you before you start reading, or as a revision exercise after you have finished the story.

Food-related words

1 Read the definitions in the box then complete the sentences below with one of the words in the correct form.

---

chafing dish a metal plate mounted above a heating device and used to cook food or keep it warm at the table
cluster a small group of things that are very close to each other
heap place things on top of each other to make a big pile
joint a large piece of meat, often cooked in an oven
laden carrying something heavy, or supporting the weight of something heavy
napkin a piece of cloth or paper used for protecting your clothes and wiping your mouth and hands when you are eating
sweetmeat a small, sweet cake or pastry

---

1 After an enormous lunch the guests were presented with a range of .... to eat with their coffee.
2 I want to buy a nice .... for lunch but I'm not sure what to get: lamb or beef.
3 Jade was late for dinner. They kept her meal warm on a ....
4 The children are going to get messy eating with their hands. Could you pass me a few ....?
5 The cupboard shelf almost collapsed because it was so heavily .... with tins, jars and bottles.
6 The fruit looked delicious: big bunches of bananas and .... of grapes hanging in the window.
7 They .... up the chocolates on a big plate to look like a pyramid.

Military vocabulary

2 Read the extracts. Which words in bold refer to a) people b) sounds c) military equipment d) a way of marching?

> *Despite the distant **cannonading** and the **bugle-calls** at the corners of the streets, that whole ancient quarter ... retained its peaceful aspect.*

> *It was really pleasant to see the little white cap dodge about amid the **helmets** and **bayonets**.*

> ***Wards** of the Republic passed **at the double-quick**, singing.*

> *Half an hour later they were all captured by **troops** of the line, and were sent off to join a long **column** of prisoners about to start for Versailles.*

> *The **column** moved off between two rows of **chasseurs**.*

> *He reviewed in his mind that unlucky day ... the humiliation, the insults, and the blows with the **butts** of **muskets**.*

3 Now check your answers with the definitions below.

at the double-quick very quickly
bayonet a long sharp blade that is fixed onto the end of a long gun
bugle a metal musical instrument used by the army to show that an activity is about to begin or end
butt the end of the handle of a gun
cannonade fire heavy guns continuously
chasseur *French:* a type of soldier
column a long line of people or vehicles moving together
helmet a hard hat that you wear to protect your head
musket a type of long gun used by soldiers before the invention of the rifle
troops soldiers, especially in large numbers
ward someone, especially a child, who is officially being looked after by someone who is not their parents, such as the government

Verbs of movement

The story describes the action of the main characters and the many people in the Paris streets in a lot of detail. Colourful verbs are used, especially to describe the way people walk.

4 Read the definitions in the box. Then use one of the verbs in the correct form to replace *walk* in the sentences below (1–8).

dodge avoid someone by moving quickly, so that they do not hit you
march walk in a group matching the speed and movements of the other people
scatter if a group of people or animals scatter, they move away in different directions
slip if you slip, your feet slide accidentally and you lose your balance or fall over
strut walk in an especially confident and proud way
trail move slowly and in a tired or unhappy way, often so that you are a short distance behind other people
tramp walk slowly for a long distance
trot walk with short quick steps, usually applies to an animal

1 As the soldiers **walked** past the palace, they turned to the President and saluted.
2 Everyone was walking in the opposite direction so that he had to **walk** left and right to prevent himself from bumping into them.
3 In spring the male birds **walk** in front of the females trying to get their attention.
4 The beginner skaters were easy to identify as they **walked** on the ice.
5 She went into the last shop, her husband **walking** behind with the bags of shopping.
6 The explorers **walked** along through the snow, very tired, gradually getting closer to the Pole.
7 The dog **walked** behind its owner as fast as its little legs could carry it.
8 When the police finally arrived, the crowd of protesters **walked** quickly from the square.

Strong emotions

5 Read the definitions in the box, then choose the best word to complete the sentences (1–13).

anxious worried because you think something bad might happen
beside yourself unable to think clearly because you are very angry, upset or excited
exasperated extremely annoyed and impatient because things are not happening in the way that you want
fatigue a feeling of being extremely tired, either physically or mentally
humiliation the unhappy and ashamed feeling that you get when something embarrassing happens

in a whirl confused and disorganized
indignation anger about an unfair situation or about someone's unfair behaviour
longing a strong feeling of wanting someone or something
lose your head become so upset or worried that you stop thinking clearly or behaving in a sensible way
merriment laughter and fun
obstinate not willing to be reasonable and change your plans, ideas or behaviour
scandalised very shocked
wrath *formal:* very great anger

1 Children's sleep problems cause parents *wrath/fatigue* and worry.
2 He feared the *merriment/wrath* of his employer.
3 He was still *in a whirl/scandalised* with all the music and lights.
4 I can see now that my **obstinate/longing** refusal caused problems for everyone.
5 I was so *anxious/scandalised* with anger that I forgot to post the letter.
6 I'm afraid at that point I *lost my head/exasperated* and panicked.
7 It takes her an hour just to put her shoes on. You'd *lose your head/ be exasperated*, too!
8 Jean ached with a *humiliation/longing* to return home and see her family again.
9 People are naturally *anxious/obstinate* about these tests.
10 Polly had done all the work but got none of the recognition. Her face burned with *indignation/fatigue*.
11 Sounds of *merriment/indignation* and laughter came from the party downstairs.
12 They were *scandalised/in a whirl* when they saw the graffiti all over their car.
13 I doubt he would risk further public *merriment/humiliation*.

Main themes

Before you read the story, you may want to think about some of its main themes. The questions will help you think about the story as you are reading it for the first time. There is more discussion of the main themes in the *Literary analysis* section after the story.

The individual and society

The story takes place at a time of great social and political change in France. It describes the impact these historic events have on ordinary people's lives.

6 As you read the story, think about the following questions:

a) In what ways are the main characters following their normal routines?

b) Are the characters aware of the events going on around them?

c) How do the main characters feel about what is happening in Paris?

Personal concerns

The story explores the concerns of the two main characters; that is, the things that are important to them. Their concerns are compared with those of other people in Paris on that day and the wider world of French politics.

7 As you read the story, ask yourself:

a) What is the main thing Monsieur Bonnicar is interested in? Why?

b) What about the apprentice – what is his main concern?

The Little Pies

by Alphonse Daudet

THAT morning, which was a Sunday, Sureau, the pastry-cook on Rue Turenne, called his apprentice and said to him:

"Here are Monsieur Bonnicar's little pies; go and take them to him and come back at once. It seems that the Versaillais[1] have entered Paris."

The little fellow[2], who understood nothing about politics, put the smoking hot pies in the dish, the dish in a white napkin, and balancing the whole upon his cap, started off on a run for Île St. Louis, where M. Bonnicar lived. It was a magnificent morning, one of those bright, sunny May mornings which fill the fruit-shops with clusters of cherries and bunches of lilac. Despite the distant cannonading and the bugle-calls at the corners of the streets, that whole ancient **quarter** of the Marais retained its peaceful aspect. There was Sunday in the air; bands of children in the yards, tall girls playing battledore[3] in front of the doors, and that little white silhouette, trotting along in the middle of the deserted roadway, **amid** a pleasant odour of hot pies, put the finishing touch of **artlessness** and Sunday merriment to that morning of battle. All the life of the quarter seemed to have betaken itself to Rue de Rivoli. Cannon were being drawn thither[4] and barricades thrown up; groups of people at every step. National Guardsmen full of business. But the little pastry-cook did not lose his head. Those children are so accustomed to walking in the midst[5] of crowds and the uproar of the street! On saints' days and holidays, when the streets are so crowded, early

1 government soldiers
2 *old-fashioned*: a man
3 an early form of badminton
4 *old-fashioned*: 'to that place'
5 *formal*: if you are in the midst of something, it is all around you

in the year, and on Sundays, they have the most running to do; so that revolutions hardly surprise them.

It was really pleasant to see the little white cap dodge about amid the helmets and bayonets, avoiding collisions, maintaining its equilibrium[6], sometimes very rapidly, sometimes with a compulsory slowness in which one was conscious still of a longing to run. What difference did the battle make to him? The important thing was to arrive at Bonnicar's on the stroke of noon, and to run away at once with the little fee which awaited him on the small table in the reception-room.

Suddenly there was a terrible pressure in the crowd, and wards of the Republic passed at the double-quick, singing. They were lads of twelve to fifteen years, arrayed in helmets, red belts, and high boots; as proud of being disguised as soldiers as when they run about on Mardi Gras[7] with paper caps and a strip of a fancy pink umbrella, in the mud of the **boulevards**. This time, in the midst of the crowd, the little pastry-cook had much difficulty in keeping his balance; but his dish and he had slipped so many times upon the ice, had played so many games of hop-scotch on the **sidewalk**, that the little pies escaped with a fright. Unluckily that excitement, those songs, those red belts, combined with admiration and curiosity, **aroused** in the apprentice the desire to march a little way in such goodly[8] company; and passing the Hôtel de Ville[9] and the bridges leading to Île St. Louis without noticing them, he found himself carried I know not whither[10], in the dust and the wind of that wild march.

II

FOR at least twenty-five years, it had been the custom of the Bonnicars to eat little pies on Sunday. At precisely twelve o'clock, when the whole family, great and small, was assembled in the salon, a sharp and merry ring at the bell would cause them all to say:

6 *formal*: balance
7 a celebration with parties and marches in the streets
8 *old-fashioned*: of considerable size, large
9 the town hall
10 *old-fashioned*: 'to which place'

"Ah! There's the pastry-cook."

Thereupon[11], with a great moving of chairs, the **rustle** of Sunday clothes, the expansive joy of laughing children about the well-laden table, all those happy bourgeois would take their places around the little pies, symmetrically heaped upon the silver chafing-dish.

That day the bell remained dumb. Monsieur Bonnicar, scandalised, looked at his clock, an old clock surmounted[12] by a stuffed **heron**, which had never in its life **gained** or lost. The children yawned at the windows, watching the corner of the street where the apprentice usually appeared. Conversation **languished**, and hunger, which noon with its twelve strokes digs in the stomach, made the dining room look very large and very **dismal**, despite the antique silver plate glistening on the damask cloth; and the napkins all about, folded in the shape of little stiff white horns.

Several times already the old cook had come to whisper in her master's ear: the joint burned, the peas cooked too much. But Monsieur Bonnicar was obstinately determined not to take his place at the table without the little pies; and, furiously angry with Sureau, he resolved to go himself to see what such an unheard-of delay could mean. As he went out, **brandishing** his **cane**, hot with indignation, some neighbours warned him:

"Take care, Monsieur Bonnicar; they say that the Versaillais have entered Paris."

He refused to listen to anything, even to the cannonading which came from Neuilly, even to the alarm guns from the Hôtel de Ville, which shook all the windows in the quarter.

"Oh! that Sureau! that Sureau!"

And in his excitement he talked to himself, fancied[13] himself already in the middle of the shop, striking the floor with his cane, making the mirrors in the show-window and the plates of sweetmeats **tremble**. The barricade on Pont Louis Philippe cut his wrath in two. There were some confederates there, of

11 *formal*: immediately after that
12 *formal, unusual*: with something on top
13 *literary*: believe or imagine that something is true

ferocious mien[14], strutting about in the sun on the unpaved ground.

"Where are you going, citizen?"

The citizen explained, but the story of the little pies seemed suspicious, especially as Monsieur Bonnicar had on his fine Sunday coat, his gold **spectacles**, and wore every appearance of an old reactionary.

"He's a spy," said the confederates; "we must send him to Rigault[15]."

Whereupon[16] four enthusiasts, who were not sorry to leave the barricade, pushed the unfortunate, exasperated man before them with the butts of their guns.

I know not how they **accomplished** it, but half an hour later they were all captured by troops of the line, and were sent off to join a long column of prisoners about to start for Versailles. Monsieur Bonnicar protested more and more loudly, brandished his cane, told his story for the hundredth time. Unfortunately the fable about the little pies seemed so absurd, so incredible in the midst of that intense excitement, that the officers simply laughed.

"That's all right, that's all right, old fellow. You can explain at Versailles."

And through the Champs Élysées[17] still white with the smoke of the firing, the column moved off between two rows of chasseurs.

III

THE prisoners marched five by five, in close, compact ranks. To prevent the escort from being separated, they were obliged to walk arm in arm; and the long human flock, tramping along through the dust of the road, made a noise like a heavy shower.

The unfortunate Bonnicar thought that he was dreaming. **Perspiring**, **puffing**, beside himself with alarm and fatigue,

---

14 *formal*: the usual expression on someone's face, or their usual way of behaving

15 one of the leaders in the Paris Commune

16 *literary*: something which happens just after or because of something that has been mentioned

17 a long avenue in Paris

he trailed along at the end of the column, between two old **hags** who smelt of petroleum and brandy; and from the words, "Pastry-cook, little pies," which constantly occurred in his imprecations[18], everybody about him thought that he had gone mad. In truth, the poor man's head was in a whirl. When they went up or down hill, and the ranks of the escort separated a little, he actually imagined that he saw, in the dust which filled the gaps, the white jacket and cap of the little apprentice at Sureau's! And that happened ten times on the road. That little white flash passed before his eyes as if to **mock** at him; then disappeared amid the swell of uniforms, blouses, and rags.

At last, at nightfall, they arrived at Versailles; and when the crowd saw that old fellow with spectacles, **dilapidated**, dust-covered, and **haggard**, everybody agreed that he had the face of a villain. They said:

"It's Felix Pyat – no, it is Delescleuze."

The chasseurs of the escort had much difficulty in landing him safe and sound in the court of the orangery[19]. Not until then could the poor flock scatter, stretch itself out on the ground, and **draw breath**. There were some who slept, others who swore, others who coughed, others who wept; but Bonnicar neither slept nor wept. Seated on a step, with his head in his hands, three-fourths dead with hunger, shame, and fatigue, he reviewed in his mind that unlucky day, his departure from his house, his anxious guests, that meal delayed until evening and still awaiting him; and the humiliation, the insults, and the **blows** with the butts of muskets, all because of an unpunctual pastry-cook.

"Monsieur Bonnicar, here's your little pies!" suddenly said a voice close beside him; and the good man, raising his head, was greatly surprised to see the little apprentice from Sureau's, who had been arrested with the wards of the Republic, remove his cap, and hand him the dish which was concealed under his white apron. Thus it was that, despite the riot and his imprisonment, Monsieur Bonnicar had his little pies on that Sunday as on others.

18 *very formal*: an offensive word that you say when you are angry
19 a building in Versailles

Post-reading activities

Understanding the story

Use these questions to help you check that you have understood the story.

1 Approximately how old is the apprentice?
2 How busy are the streets immediately surrounding the pastry shop in the Marais area? Why?
3 What is the atmosphere like in the Rue de Rivoli?
4 What happens that distracts the apprentice from his work?
5 Why are the little pies important to the Bonnicar family?
6 What is Monsieur Bonnicar's reaction when he realizes that the pies have not arrived?
7 What do his neighbours warn him about?
8 How many times is Monsieur Bonnicar captured by soldiers? Why does he get captured each time?
9 Why don't the soldiers believe his story?
10 How does Monsieur Bonnicar feel as he marches towards Versailles?
11 What do the other prisoners think about Monsieur Bonnicar?
12 What makes him think he is going mad? Is he?
13 How has Monsieur Bonnicar's appearance changed through the day?
14 How does Monsieur Bonnicar feel when he sees the apprentice?

Language study

Grammar

Adding detail: participle clauses

The storyteller in *The Little Pies* often uses participle clauses to add detail to his descriptions. Here are two examples from the first part of the story:

*Wards of the Republic passed at the double-quick, **singing**. They were lads of twelve to fifteen years, **arrayed in helmets, red belts, and high boots**.*

Form

Participle clauses are reduced clauses. They contain a verb, but they do not usually contain a subject.

In present participle clauses we use the *-ing* form of the verb: **singing**

In past participle clauses we use the past participle: **arrayed** *in helmets, red belts, and high boots*

Present participle clauses (*-ing* clauses) replace verbs in the active.

Past participle clauses (*-ed* clauses) replace verbs in the passive.

> *Wards of the Republic sang* → *singing*
>
> *They were arrayed in helmets, red belts, and high boots* → *arrayed in helmets, red belts, and high boots*

Use

Participle clauses are mainly used in writing. They allow the writer to condense relative clauses and combine sentences.

1 Read these sentences. Notice how they have been combined in the extracts from the story. Notice which words have been omitted or changed.

> *He passed the Hôtel de Ville and the bridges leading to Île St. Louis without noticing them. He found himself carried I know not whither.*
>
> ***Passing** the Hotel de Ville and the bridges leading to Île St. Louis without noticing them, he found himself carried I know not whither.*
>
> *All those happy bourgeois would take their places around the little pies. The pies were symmetrically heaped upon the silver chafing-dish.*
>
> *All those happy bourgeois would take their places around the little pies, symmetrically **heaped** upon the silver chafing-dish.*

2 Combine the sentences below using a participle clause. The first has been done as an example.

1 *The children yawned at the windows. They watched the corner of the street.* (page 68)

   The children yawned at the windows, watching the corner of the street.

2 *Monsieur Bonnicar was scandalised. He looked at his clock* (page 68)

3 *There were some confederates there, of ferocious mien. They were strutting about in the sun on the unpaved ground.* (page 69)

4   *The long human flock tramped along through the dust of the road. It made a noise like a heavy shower.* (page 69)

....

5   *The good man raised his head. He was greatly surprised to see the little apprentice from Sureau's.* (page 70)

....

Compare your answers with the original sentences in the story.

Multiple-clause sentences

Like many texts, a feature of this story is a variety in sentence length. Some sentences in the story are short – just a few words. They are used for several reasons. For example, they can make the reader stop and think:

What difference did the battle make to him?

Or they can create a dramatic effect:

That day the bell remained dumb.

Other sentences contain many clauses, so their structure is often very complex. They may be used to set the scene, create atmosphere or to sum up a situation as they can condense a lot of details into one sentence. Look at this example. The clauses are numbered:

(1) The little fellow, (2) who understood nothing about politics, put the smoking hot pies in the dish, (3) the dish in a white napkin, and (4) balancing the whole upon his cap, (5) started off on a run for Île St. Louis, (6) where M. Bonnicar lived.

Look at how the clauses break down into short sentences:

1   The little fellow put the smoking hot pies in the dish.
2   He understood nothing about politics.
3   He put the dish in a white napkin.
4   He balanced the whole upon his cap.
5   He started off on a run for Île St. Louis.
6   M. Bonnicar lived there.

In this case, the long sentence helps to convey the way that the apprentice hurries to set off for Monsieur Bonnicar's house. Notice how commas are used to separate the various clauses and help us process the sentence as we read it.

3 Read another example. How many clauses are in this sentence? Use commas to separate the clauses where necessary. Check your answers on page 66.

There was Sunday in the air bands of children in the yards tall girls playing battledore in front of the doors and that little white silhouette trotting along in the middle of the deserted roadway amid a pleasant odour of hot pies put the finishing touch of artlessness and Sunday merriment to that morning of battle.

4 Now break the sentence down into separate sentences. Compare your sentences with the one in the story. What is the difference in the effect?

Note: Multiple-clause sentences exist in most types of authentic text, especially older literature. They can be very effective but their length and complexity can also be confusing. One way to make multiple-clause sentences easier to understand is to break them down into shorter clauses as you have done here.

Literary analysis

Plot

1 What are the main events in the plot?
2 Which of the following events are not described directly? What effect does this have on the story?
  a) The Versaillais enter Paris.
  b) Sureau sends his apprentice to the Bonnicars' house.
  c) Monsieur Bonnicar gets angry and goes out into the street.
  d) Monsieur Bonnicar is arrested.
  e) The soldiers who arrested Monsieur Bonnicar are captured (with Monsieur Bonnicar).
  f) The apprentice is arrested.
  g) The prisoners arrive at Versailles.
3 How much information are we given about the political and military events surrounding the story? What is the effect on the story?
4 What are we told about the concerns of the main characters?
5 Do you think it is important that the apprentice manages to find Monsieur Bonnicar at the end? Why/Why not?
6 What is the main message of the story? Is it still relevant in any way to today's readers?
7 What do you think happens to them next?

The role of food in the story

8   Who makes the food for the Bonnicar family? What does this tell you about them?
9   Why is Monsieur Bonnicar so angry when the pies do not arrive? What do they represent for him?
10 Why does the apprentice think that it is important to deliver the pies?
11 How important are the pies in the lives of Monsieur Bonnicar and the apprentice?

Character

12 Who is the main character, or do the apprentice and Monsieur Bonnicar share this role? Why do you think this?
13 How is the apprentice dressed? What do you think Monsieur Bonnicar is wearing?
14 What do you know about each of the main characters? Think about their age, class, educational background, character and so on.
15 Below is a list of adjectives of character. Which describe Monsieur Bonnicar? Which describe the apprentice?

angry	calm	confused
curious	distracted	forgetful
frustrated	stubborn	traditional

16 In what ways are the two characters similar?
17 Do you have any sympathy for Monsieur Bonnicar? Why/Why not? Do you think he is right to get angry?
18 What does the fact that the apprentice managed to get the pies to Monsieur Bonnicar tell you about him?
19 Make a list of the other characters in the story. Which of them are the most significant, in your opinion? Why?

Narration

20 The story is told in the third person. Do we get any impression of the storyteller? Does the storyteller offer any opinions?
21 The story begins by describing the apprentice's day before it moves to Monsieur Bonnicar's story in the second part. How would your reading experience have changed if you had read about Monsieur Bonnicar first?

22 Find the moments in the story when characters speak. How much speech is there? Think about their purpose. Find one which:
a) provides us with important information.
b) expresses the emotion of a character.
c) is part of a longer dialogue which is not quoted.
Imagine how the characters say these lines. Read them out loud.

Style

23 Read the first part of the story again. Notice how the atmosphere of Paris is described. Is the street scene described positively or negatively? What is the effect in relation to the following events in the story?

24 Read the following extracts. Notice the change of tense that takes place in both. What is this day being compared with? Why is there a change of tense?

But the little pastry-cook did not lose his head. Those children are so accustomed to walking in the midst of crowds and the uproar of the street! On saints' days and holidays, when the streets are so crowded … they have the most running to do; so that revolutions hardly surprise them.

They were lads of twelve to fifteen years, arrayed in helmets, red belts, and high boots; as proud of being disguised as soldiers as when they run about on Mardi Gras with paper caps and a strip of a fancy pink umbrella, in the mud of the boulevards.

25 Look again at the paragraph beginning: 'That day the bell remained dumb' (page 68). Notice the way that the sentences focus on the different elements in the room: Monsieur Bonnicar, the objects, the children. Imagine the scene were recreated for the cinema. What effect does the language create?

26 Read the sentence below. Notice how the writer uses commas to separate items on a list:

Unluckily that excitement, those songs, those red belts, combined with admiration and curiosity, aroused in the apprentice the desire to march a little way in such goodly company.

Find more examples of this listing technique. What emotions are being described or transmitted at these points in the story?

Guidance to the above literary terms, answer keys to all the exercises and activities, plus a wealth of other reading-practice material, can be found at: www.macmillanenglish.com/readers.

A Piece of Steak

by Jack London

About the author

John Griffith London was born in San Francisco in 1876. His mother, Flora Wellman, was a music teacher from a wealthy background. She was not married to the man who was probably Jack's father – the journalist, lawyer and astrologer, William Chaney – so the young writer took the name of his stepfather, John London. In his teens, the young John London became known as Jack.

Flora and John were poor, and Jack's childhood was hard. He had little formal education, and started work when he was very young to bring in extra money. By the age of fourteen Jack was working sixteen-hour shifts at a local factory. For several years the young writer went from job to job and place to place, taking any work he could, including deep-sea fishing, shovelling coal, doing manual work in factories, even collecting oysters illegally in Oakland Bay. In between, he travelled. His journey on a freight train across America provided much of the material for his partly autobiographical book, *The Road* (1907).

Returning to San Francisco when his stepfather died, Jack took a job in a laundry to earn enough money to support his mother. Still writing, but as yet unpublished, he studied at the same time, gaining a place at the University of Berkeley in California, though he did not complete his degree. At the age of just twenty-five his first short story was published. It was an immediate success, and after years of hard work and poverty, London went on to become one of the highest paid, and most celebrated writers of his generation.

By the time he was thirty, London had produced three of his most famous novels – *The Call of the Wild* (1903), *Sea Wolf* (1904) and *White Fang* (1906), all of which examined the power of nature and instinct. He had also been married, had two children and got divorced in that time. London married again to Charmian Kittredge, with whom he travelled widely. As famous for his adventures as his writing, London was charismatic and good-looking, telling stories based on his experience. In addition to his writing, he also worked as a war correspondent, rode horses on his ranch in California, hosted extravagant parties and sailed across the South Pacific with Charmian.

London loved boxing. As well as watching many professional fights, he was a keen boxer himself, taking any opportunity to fight with people he would meet on his travels. He even boxed with Charmian: while sailing, they used to practise on the boat in the mornings. She was a good boxing partner because he felt he could not attack a lady, so he focused on his defence instead. London wrote several stories about boxing. Jimmy Britt, a lightweight boxer of the time, said, after reading one of the stories, that he would happily accept London as a referee for one of his boxing matches.

London's work ethic continued throughout his life, and his commitment to writing one thousand words a day meant that he produced a great deal of work – his subjects and themes were adventure and difficulty. He continued to work hard and play hard until his death in 1916 at the age of just forty, from kidney failure related to his heavy drinking. He left eighteen volumes of short stories, nineteen novels, seven non-fiction books, and hundreds of published articles, essays, and reviews.

Details about the life and character of Jack London are controversial, but what is certain is that he led a full life, full of travel and adventure, experiencing and writing about what he called 'big moments of living'.

About the story

A *Piece of Steak* first appeared in 1909 in *The Saturday Evening Post*. This was one of the most popular magazines in America at the time; its readers knew London's work well because his novel, *The Call of the Wild*, had been printed in the same publication six years earlier. Even though the short story only took him eighteen days to write, London made $500 from it – a lot of money in those days.

Like *The Little Pies* in this collection, A *Piece of Steak* is part of a movement in literature called Naturalism, which tries to understand the difficulties of life in a cruel and unequal society.

Background information

Food in the story: paying for food

Poor families often didn't have enough money to buy the food they needed. In modern society it is normal for people who need money to organize credit with their bank, that is, to agree to receive money from them and pay for it later. In the past, it was common to arrange credit directly with tradesmen such as butchers and other shopkeepers, so that people could buy food from their shops when they needed it, but pay for it days or weeks later. Many families ran up bills with local shops: the tradesman kept a list of what they owed, so they could continue to shop there. If a customer had owed the shop money for a long time and payment was late, or if the tradesman did not believe a person could pay it back, he might refuse to give them credit.

Another form of credit could come from a person's employer, who might advance them their pay. This means they would give them their pay before the usual time.

There is a recipe for Australian barbecued steak with sauce on page 190.

The boxing business

Boxing is one of the oldest sports, and is a big business for the people who organize fights, promote fighters, write about boxing in the sporting columns of newspapers, and nowadays, show matches on television. Boxers are just one part of the industry; they are also known as prize-fighters or pugilists.

A boxer may also have a backer: someone who gives them money to support them in their training and buys things that they need. Boxers need to practise fighting, so they use another boxer as a sparring partner.

Fight promoters arrange matches by putting one boxer up against another. The promoter pays the boxers what is known as the purse. The amount that each fighter will get is fixed before the fight and depends on whether they win or lose. The 'winner's end' of the purse is typically much more than the 'loser's end'.

The boxing match

Before a fight, the boxers get dressed and put on their gloves in the dressing room. To get to the ring, they walk through the audience along an aisle, or passage between the seats. As well as spectators who pay to watch the fight, journalists covering the fight for their newspapers will also be seated in a special section of the 'house' called the press box. The fight takes place on a square platform surrounded by ropes known as the ring. A referee is also present in the ring. His job is to make sure that the boxers obey the rules.

A boxing match, or bout, is divided into shorter rounds, which are normally three minutes long. Before the bout starts and between rounds, the boxers sit on stools in opposite corners of the ring. Each round starts and ends with the sound of a bell or gong, a circular metal object which makes a loud, deep noise when hit with a stick. Between rounds, the fighters are allowed to return to their corner and rest for a minute, during which their coach, and other assistants, known as seconds, can help them recover by giving them water, treating cuts and other injuries.

Types of punch

A boxer may hit his opponent in a number of different ways. There are also various ways he can defend himself from being hit.

To describe a punch in general you can use *strike*, *deliver a punch*, *throw a punch* and *land a punch*. A *hook* is a sideways hit made with the arm bent. An *upper cut* is a way of hitting someone hard on the chin or in the stomach by swinging your arm upwards. If a boxer *swings* at their opponent, they try to hit them by punching in a smooth curving movement. A boxer may wait for his opponent to throw a punch in order to exploit the opening in the opponent's position with a *counter* punch. A boxer *feints* when he pretends to punch, getting his opponent to move out of a good defensive position and so creating an opening for a real attack. Any punch may be described as *a right* or *a left*, depending on which arm is used.

Ways of defending yourself include *ducking*, or lowering your head and body quickly in order to avoid being hit, and *blocking*, where you stop your opponent's punch from hitting your head or other sensitive part of your body by putting your hands in the way. When a boxer is too tired to defend himself, he may hold on to the opponent to avoid being hit. This is called a *clinch*.

When a player is knocked to the ground, the referee counts to ten. It is sensible to stay down for as long as possible in this situation because it gives you time to recover. This is called *taking the count*. A *knockout* is a punch which results in the opponent falling on the mat and staying down for the full ten seconds. If that happens, he loses and the match is over.

Summary

It may help you to know something about what happens in the story before you read it. Don't worry, this summary does not tell you how the story ends!

Tom King is a boxer who has many years of experience in the ring and has had a lot of success in his career. He is getting old, and his long experience of fighting is visible in his broken nose and swollen ears. His battered face and body show the long-term effects that this difficult sport has had on him.

The story starts with King at home in the hours before his next match. He looks back on his glorious past as the heavyweight champion of New South Wales in Australia. He remembers when he was winning all his matches and had money to be generous with and give away. But he is no longer rich – in fact, he does not even have enough money to feed his family or himself. His wife, Lizzie, has tried to get some steak for him before the fight, but the butcher refused her credit. Unfortunately, he has already received an advance of the money that he would get if he lost the fight, so he cannot ask for more. King's meal of bread and gravy is not enough food for a man who will fight in a few hours.

He has to walk to the Gayety Club, where the match will take place, because he has no money for a taxi. His opponent that evening is a promising young boxer from New Zealand called Sandel. Despite Sandel's age, his strength and his ability to recover quickly, he is going to find that the older man is more difficult to beat than he perhaps imagines. King may be old, tired and hungry, but he knows exactly how best to fight this youngster: patiently and cleverly.

The two are fighting for different reasons. Sandel wants to impress the boxing world and advance his career, whereas King is just hoping to be able to feed himself and his family and to pay the rent. Both of them are motivated to win, but who will take home the winner's purse?

Pre-reading activities

Key vocabulary

Boxing and food terms are dealt with in the section on Background information (page 79). This section will help you familiarize yourself with more of the specific vocabulary used in the story. You may want to use it to help you before you start reading, or as a revision exercise after you have finished the story.

Poverty and wealth

Although King has no money now, he was not always poor. There are many references to money, or the lack of money, throughout the story.

1 **Read the extracts below and match the words in bold to their definitions (a–n).**

1 *He sat down by the window on a **rickety** chair.*
2 *He had managed to borrow a few **shillings** from old pals, who would have lent more only they were **hard put** themselves.*
3 *He looked around the bare room. It was all he had in the world, with the rent **overdue**, and her and the kiddies.*
4 *He had nothing to win except thirty **quid**, to pay to the **landlord** and the tradesmen.*
5 *He had done a few days' **navvy work** when he could get it.*
6 *His rough clothes were old and **slouchy**. The uppers of his shoes were too weak to carry the heavy **re-soling** that was itself of no recent date. And his cotton shirt, a cheap, two-**shilling** affair, showed a **frayed** collar.*
7 *Outside the ring he was slow-going, easy-natured, and, in his younger days, when money was **flush**, too **open-handed** for his own good.*
8 *He heard the **prosperous** chink of money on the bar … He had not a **copper** in his pocket.*
9 *The last two **ha'pennies** had gone to buy the bread.*

a) (adj) experiencing financial difficulty
b) (adj) *informal*: with a lot more money than you usually have
c) (adj) generous
d) (adj) a payment described as this should have been paid before now
e) (n) a man who owns a house, flat, or room that people can rent
f) (adj) hanging loosely with no clear shape
g) (v) repair a shoe by replacing the bottom part of it that goes under your foot

h) (n) *old-fashioned*: a coin of low value made of copper or bronze
i) (adj) rich and successful
j) (adj) likely to break if you put any weight on it, often because it is old
k) (n) *informal*: a pound in money
l) (adj) clothes like this are worn out at the edges
m) `PHRASE` hard physical work, for example building roads or railways
n) (n) small units of money that are not used in Australia now

Adjectives to describe a person's physical appearance

The two boxers in the story are quite different: King is old, heavy and tired and Sandel is much younger and fitter.

2 Read the definitions of adjectives that describe the boxers' physical state. Which describe King? Which describe Sandel?

> **burdened** carrying something heavy
> **dazzling** extremely impressive
> **grizzled** a grizzled person has grey hair and looks old
> **hulking** very large and heavy in appearance, especially in a way that seems ugly or frightening
> **lusty** healthy, strong or enthusiastic
> **shaggy** with long, thick and untidy hair
> **silken** very soft, smooth or shiny
> **sleek** smooth and shiny
> **stolid** acting or thinking in a slow, serious manner
> **supple** able to move and bend your body very easily and in a graceful way

3 Choose the correct adjective to complete the sentences.

1 The city's *burdened/stolid/hulking* official buildings serve as reminders of the awesome power of the imperial state.
2 A young, well-dressed woman with short, *grizzled/burdened/sleek* hair came into the room.
3 The grandfather came to the door, *dazzling/silken/grizzled* and bent.
4 Both athletes showed such a high standard of play. Moments of the match were *dazzling/lusty/hulking*.
5 He was slower than the others, *silken/burdened/grizzled* by his enormous rucksack.
6 I do stretching exercises every day to keep myself *stolid/supple/sleek*.

7   It was one of those big, **shaggy/supple/stolid** dogs, his eyes hidden under all that hair.
8   The man's **stolid/supple/sleek** face revealed nothing. Was he too stupid or too clever to react?

Expressing aggression

The writer uses many words to express aggression and describe fighting.

4   Read the words below and categorize them according to their part of speech: noun, verb, adjective or adverb.

> **animus** a strong feeling of disliking someone or something
> **brawl** a noisy fight in a public place
> **brutish** violent and cruel
> **fierce** involving a lot of force or energy
> **hammer and tongs** with a lot of energy and enthusiasm
> **ill-will** a strong feeling that you dislike someone and wish them harm
> **insurgence** the act of fighting against someone in authority in order to take control
> **merciless** without mercy or compassion
> **onslaught** a powerful attack
> **pick a quarrel** start a fight or argument with someone
> **rally** come together again in order to continue fighting after a defeat
> **retaliate** do something harmful or unpleasant to someone because they have done something harmful or unpleasant to you

5   Complete the sentences with words from 4 in the correct form.

1   Angry demonstrators threw rocks and firebombs. The police .... with tear gas.
2   Listen, I don't want to .... with you, I think we can talk about this without fighting.
3   The area around the football stadium is famous for street fighting and pub ....
4   Cleveland were losing but .... late in the game to beat Detroit 5–4.
5   The decorators have been working .... over the last week to get the house ready on time.
6   Football should not tolerate such .... behaviour, on the pitch or off it.

Parts of the body

Boxing has been described as the most physically demanding sport. The story describes in detail how boxing affects different parts of the fighters' bodies.

6 Complete the definitions for the parts of the body using the words in the box.

chest	eyes	fingers	arm	body
teeth	hand	heart	skin (x2)	

1 **arteries** and **veins** the tubes in your body that carry blood from your .... to the rest of your body

2 **biceps** the muscles between your shoulder and your elbow on the front of your ....

3 **brow** *literary*: forehead, the part of your face above your ....

4 **fist** your hand when your .... are closed tightly

5 **jaw** the lower part of your face that includes your chin and your bottom ....

6 **knuckles** the parts of your .... where your fingers can bend or where they join your hand

7 **lids** the pieces of .... that cover your eyes when they are closed

8 **pores** the very small holes in your .... that sweat can pass through

9 **ribs** the long curved bones that are in your .... and protect your heart and lungs

10 **solar plexus** collection of nerves in the front part of your ...., behind your stomach, that is painful if you are hit hard there

Physical processes

7 Complete the text with some of the words from 6. Use the verbs in bold and their definitions below to help you.

He was really hot now; sweat was **oozing** from his (1)............................
His heart had been **pumping** hard for almost an hour and he could feel the blood **surging** through his (2)........................... His chest **heaving**, the lungs felt as though they might **burst** with this mighty effort as they **swelled** and **shrank** up and down beneath his (3)........................... There was pain in his muscles, particularly his left arm, where his (4)........................... kept **cramping**. He could see his opponent just over his shoulder. He **clenched** his (5)...........................
in determination, his whole body **quivering** with this one last effort.

> **surge** move forwards as a large mass very quickly
> **pump** move with a regular action that makes a liquid or gas move
> **burst** if something bursts, it breaks suddenly because there is too much pressure inside it
> **ooze** if a thick liquid oozes, a small amount of it flows out slowly
> **quiver** shake with short quick movements
> **shrink** become smaller in size
> **swell** become larger than normal
> **clench** if you do this to a part of your body such as your hand or your mouth, you close it tightly
> **cramp** when a tired muscle does this, it becomes very tight, causing sudden severe pain
> **heave** move up and down with large regular movements

Injuries and medical problems

8 Read the words below and their definitions. Which are used to talk about:

a) injuries to the head?
b) permanent injuries?

> **unconsciousness** a condition similar to sleep in which you do not see, feel or think, usually because you are injured
> **swollen** an area of your body that is swollen has increased in size as a result of an injury or an illness
> **maim** injure someone seriously, often so that they can no longer use a part of their body
> **harm** injure, damage or have a bad effect on someone or something
> **gash** a long deep cut in your skin or in the surface of something

distension if a vein or artery suffers from distension, it stretches too much so that it cannot return to its normal size

dazed unable to think clearly because you are tired or have been hit on the head

cauliflower ears a medical condition in which someone's ear is swollen, usually because of an injury

bleared not able to see clearly, for example because you are tired (usually *bleary*)

batter hit something very hard several times

Verbs of movement

9 **Read the following extracts. Which of the verbs in bold describe a movement a boxer is likely to make when he has lots of energy and is in control?**

1 *His legs were like lead, and they **dragged** visibly under him;*

2 *He **leaped** lightly to the raised platform and ducked through the ropes to his corner*

3 *He **lurched** forward toward King in the hope of effecting a clinch and gaining more time.*

4 *From the impact of the blow, Tom King himself **reeled** back and nearly fell.*

5 *With the gong, Sandel **rushed**, making a show of freshness.*

6 *Always were these youngsters rising up in the boxing game, **springing** through the ropes and shouting their defiance*

7 *Sandel **swayed**, but did not fall, **staggering** back to the ropes and holding on.*

8 *There had been no time for him to fall. The audience saw him **totter** and his knees give, and then saw him recover.*

Now check your ideas with the definitions below.

drag pull part of your body along the ground because you are injured
leap jump somewhere suddenly and quickly
lurch move suddenly in a way that is not smooth or controlled
reel move backwards in a way that is not steady
rush move quickly towards someone or something, especially in order to attack them
spring jump or move in a particular direction, quickly and with a lot of energy
stagger walk in an uncontrolled way, as if you are going to fall over
sway move or swing gently from side to side
totter stand or move in a way that is not steady

A note about spoken language

The author imitates the working-class accent of the characters in the way he writes the dialogue. Non-standard spelling and grammar is used to show the way that Tom and Lizzie King speak and this may make it harder to understand at first. You will understand it better if you know some of the conventions for imitating speech.

Omitted sounds in a word or phrase are indicated with an apostrophe. For example, in King's accent the 'h' sound at the start of words is often not pronounced, so *him* is written *'im*. Other examples include *g'wan* for *go on*, *'ud* for *would* and *an'* for *and*. Another convention is to use different vowels in words to show the regional accent, such as when *your* becomes *yer*, *what* becomes *wot* and *one* is written *un*.

Non-standard grammar is also used to imitate speech. You will read the common negative *ain't* instead of *are not* and *have not*, for example.

Try to understand this sentence from the story:

> *"As how 'e was thinkin' Sandel ud do ye to-night, an' as how yer score was comfortable big as it was."* (*comfortable big = big enough*)

Main themes

Before you read the story, you may want to think about some of its main themes. The questions will help you think about the story as you are reading it for the first time. There is more discussion of the main themes in the *Literary analysis* section after the story.

Poverty

The story is set in Australia during a year of drought, a period of time when there is little rain and the crops die, so food becomes expensive. The Kings are a poor family.

10 While you read, think about these questions:

a) What different ways does Tom King have to make money for his family?

b) What prevents him from earning money this way?

Paying your debts

The story explores the theme of owing and repaying, the idea that you can borrow money and other things for a time, but that at some point in the future you have to pay it back.

11 As you read the story, consider:

a) Who does King owe money to? How can he pay them back?
b) What else does he owe? Why?

Youth and age

The story places special emphasis on the difference in age between the two boxers. It describes the problems experienced as people get older as well as the strengths that are gained by ageing.

12 As you read the story, think about the following questions:

a) What are the negative effects of ageing on King's performance in the ring?
b) Are there any positive effects? What are they?
c) Now he is older, does he have any regrets? What are they?

A Piece of Steak

by Jack London

With the last morsel of bread Tom King wiped his plate clean of the last particle of flour **gravy** and chewed the resulting mouthful in a slow and meditative way. When he arose from the table, he was oppressed by the feeling that he was distinctly hungry. Yet he alone had eaten. The two children in the other room had been sent early to bed in order that in sleep they might forget they had gone supperless. His wife had touched nothing, and had sat silently and watched him with solicitous[1] eyes. She was a thin, worn woman of the working-class, though signs of an earlier prettiness were not wanting[2] in her face. The flour for the gravy she had borrowed from the neighbour across the hall. The last two ha'pennies had gone to buy the bread.

He sat down by the window on a rickety chair that protested under his weight, and quite mechanically he put his pipe in his mouth and dipped into the side pocket of his coat. The absence of any tobacco made him aware of his action, and, with a **scowl** for his forgetfulness, he put the pipe away. His movements were slow, almost hulking, as though he were burdened by the heavy weight of his muscles. He was a solid-bodied, stolid-looking man, and his appearance did not suffer from being overprepossessing[3]. His rough clothes were old and slouchy. The uppers of his shoes were too weak to carry the heavy re-soling that was itself of no recent date. And his cotton shirt, a cheap, two-shilling affair, showed a frayed collar and **ineradicable** paint **stains**.

But it was Tom King's face that advertised him unmistakably for what he was. It was the face of a typical prize-fighter; of one who had put in long years of service in the squared ring and,

1 *formal*: showing you care about someone's health, feelings, safety etc
2 *formal*: missing
3 *unusual*: very attractive or impressive

by that means, developed and emphasized all the marks of the fighting beast. It was distinctly a lowering[4] countenance[5], and, that no feature of it might escape notice, it was clean-shaven. The lips were shapeless and constituted a mouth **harsh** to excess, that was like a gash in his face. The jaw was aggressive, brutal, heavy. The eyes, slow of movement and heavy-lidded, were almost expressionless under the shaggy, indrawn brows. **Sheer** animal that he was, the eyes were the most animal-like feature about him. They were sleepy, lion-like – the eyes of a fighting animal. The forehead slanted quickly back to the hair, which, clipped close, showed every bump of a villainous[6]-looking head. A nose twice broken and **moulded** variously by countless blows, and a cauliflower ear, permanently swollen and distorted to twice its size, completed his **adornment**, while the beard, fresh-shaven as it was, sprouted in the skin and gave the face a blue-black stain.

Altogether, it was the face of a man to be afraid of in a dark alley or lonely place. And yet Tom King was not a criminal, nor had he ever done anything criminal. Outside of brawls, common to his walk in life, he had harmed no one. Nor had he ever been known to pick a quarrel. He was a professional, and all the fighting brutishness of him was reserved for his professional appearances. Outside the ring he was slow-going, easy-natured, and, in his younger days, when money was flush, too open-handed for his own good. He **bore no grudges** and had few enemies. Fighting was a business with him. In the ring he struck to hurt, struck to maim, struck to destroy; but there was no animus in it. It was a plain business proposition. Audiences assembled and paid for the spectacle of men knocking each other out. The winner took the big end of the purse. When Tom King faced the Woolloomoolloo Gouger, twenty years before, he knew that the Gouger's jaw was only four months healed after having been broken in a Newcastle bout. And he had played for that jaw and broken it again in the ninth round, not because he

4 *unusual*: looking sullen or angry
5 *literary*: your face, or the expression on your face
6 *literary*: evil

bore the Gouger any ill-will, but because that was the surest way to put the Gouger out and win the big end of the purse. Nor had the Gouger borne him any ill-will for it. It was the game, and both knew the game and played it.

Tom King had never been a talker, and he sat by the window, **morosely** silent, staring at his hands. The veins stood out on the backs of the hands, large and swollen; and the knuckles, smashed and battered and malformed, testified to the use to which they had been put. He had never heard that a man's life was the life of his arteries, but well he knew the meaning of those big upstanding veins. His heart had pumped too much blood through them at top pressure. They no longer did the work. He had stretched the elasticity out of them, and with their distension had passed his endurance[7]. He tired easily now. No longer could he do a fast twenty rounds, hammer and tongs, fight, fight, fight, from gong to gong, with fierce rally on top of fierce rally, beaten to the ropes and in turn beating his opponent to the ropes, and rallying fiercest and fastest of all in that last, twentieth round, with the house on its feet and **yelling**, himself rushing, striking, ducking, raining showers of blows upon[8] showers of blows and receiving showers of blows in return, and all the time the heart faithfully pumping the surging blood through the adequate veins. The veins, swollen at the time, had always shrunk down again, though each time, **imperceptibly** at first, not quite – remaining just a **trifle** larger than before. He stared at them and at his battered knuckles, and, for the moment, caught a vision of the youthful excellence of those hands before the first knuckle had been smashed on the head of Benny Jones, otherwise known as the Welsh Terror.

The impression of his hunger came back on him.

"Blimey[9], but couldn't I go a piece of steak!" he **muttered** aloud, clenching his huge fists and spitting out a smothered oath[10].

7   His arteries had become weaker and were permanently damaged which meant that he wasn't as strong as he used to be.

8   *formal*: on

9   *informal British and Australian English*: used for expressing surprise

10 *old-fashioned*: something offensive that you say when you are angry

"I tried both Burke's an' Sawley's," his wife said half apologetically.

"An' they wouldn't?" he demanded.

"Not a ha'penny. Burke said –" She **faltered**.

"G'wan! Wot'd he say?"

"As how 'e was thinkin' Sandel ud do ye to-night, an' as how yer score was comfortable big as it was.[11]"

Tom King grunted, but did not reply. He was busy thinking of the bull terrier[12] he had kept in his younger days to which he had fed steaks without end. Burke would have given him credit for a thousand steaks – then. But times had changed. Tom King was getting old; and old men, fighting before second-rate clubs, couldn't expect to run bills of any size with the tradesmen.

He had got up in the morning with a **longing** for a piece of steak, and the longing had not abated. He had not had a fair training for this fight. It was a drought year in Australia, times were hard, and even the most irregular work was difficult to find. He had had no sparring partner, and his food had not been of the best nor always sufficient. He had done a few days' navvy work when he could get it, and he had run around the Domain in the early mornings to get his legs in shape. But it was hard, training without a partner and with a wife and two kiddies that must be fed. Credit with the tradesmen had undergone very slight expansion when he was matched with Sandel. The secretary of the Gayety Club had advanced him three pounds – the loser's end of the purse – and beyond that had refused to go. Now and again he had managed to borrow a few shillings from old pals, who would have lent more only that it was a drought year and they were hard put themselves. No – and there was no use in disguising the fact – his training had not been satisfactory. He should have had better food and no worries. Besides, when a man is forty, it is harder to get into condition than when he is twenty.

"What time is it, Lizzie?" he asked.

11 Burke thinks that Sandel will win the fight and isn't ready to give more credit as their debt is big enough already.

12 a type of dog

His wife went across the hall to inquire, and came back.

"Quarter before eight."

"They'll be startin' the first bout in a few minutes," he said. "Only a try-out[13]. Then there's a four-round spar 'tween Dealer Wells an' Gridley, an' a ten-round go 'tween Starlight an' some sailor bloke[14]. I don't come on for over an hour."

At the end of another silent ten minutes, he rose to his feet.

"Truth is, Lizzie, I ain't had proper trainin'."

He reached for his hat and started for the door. He did not offer to kiss her – he never did on going out – but on this night she dared to kiss him, throwing her arms around him and **compelling** him to bend down to her face. She looked quite small against the massive **bulk** of the man.

"Good luck, Tom," she said. "You gotter do 'im."

"Ay, I gotter do 'im," he repeated. "That's all there is to it. I jus' gotter do 'im."

He laughed with an attempt at heartiness, while she pressed more closely against him. Across her shoulders he looked around the bare room. It was all he had in the world, with the rent overdue, and her and the kiddies. And he was leaving it to go out into the night to get meat for his mate and **cubs** – not like a modern working-man going to his machine grind, but in the old, primitive, royal, animal way, by fighting for it.

"I gotter do 'im," he repeated, this time a hint of desperation in his voice. "If it's a win, it's thirty quid – an' I can pay all that's owin', with a lump o' money left over. If it's a lose, I get naught – not even a penny for me to ride home on the tram. The secretary's give all that's comin' from a loser's end. Good-bye, old woman. I'll come straight home if it's a win."

"An' I'll be waitin' up," she called to him along the hall.

It was full two miles to the Gayety, and as he walked along he remembered how in his palmy[15] days – he had once been the heavyweight champion of New South Wales – he would have ridden in a **cab** to the fight, and how, most likely, some heavy

13 *sport*: a test to see whether someone is good enough
14 *informal British and Australian English*: a man
15 *unusual*: successful and prosperous, especially in the past

backer would have paid for the cab and ridden with him. There were Tommy Burns and that Yankee nigger[16], Jack Johnson – they rode about in motor-cars. And he walked! And, as any man knew, a hard two miles was not the best preliminary to a fight. He was an old un, and the world did not wag well with old uns[17]. He was good for nothing now except navvy work, and his broken nose and swollen ear were against him even in that. He found himself wishing that he had learned a trade. It would have been better in the long run. But no one had told him, and he knew, deep down in his heart, that he would not have listened if they had. It had been so easy. Big money – sharp, glorious fights – periods of rest and **loafing** in between – a following of eager **flatterers**, the slaps on the back, the shakes of the hand, the toffs[18] glad to buy him a drink for the privilege of five minutes' talk – and the glory of it, the yelling houses, the **whirlwind** finish, the referee's "King wins!" and his name in the sporting columns next day.

Those had been times! But he realized now, in his slow, ruminating way, that it was the old uns he had been putting away. He was Youth, rising; and they were Age, sinking. No wonder it had been easy – they with their swollen veins and battered knuckles and **weary** in the bones of them from the long battles they had already fought. He remembered the time he put out old Stowsher Bill, at Rush-Cutters Bay, in the eighteenth round, and how old Bill had cried afterward in the dressing-room like a baby. Perhaps old Bill's rent had been overdue. Perhaps he'd had at home a missus an' a couple of kiddies. And perhaps Bill, that very day of the fight, had had a hungering for a piece of steak. Bill had fought **game** and taken incredible punishment. He could see now, after he had gone through the mill himself, that Stowsher Bill had fought for a bigger **stake**, that night twenty years ago, than had young Tom King, who had fought for glory and easy money. No wonder Stowsher Bill had cried afterward in the dressing-room.

16 *old-fashioned*: a black person – now an extremely offensive word
17 *unusual*: the world was not kind to old people
18 *informal old-fashioned*: someone from a high social class

Well, a man had only so many fights in him, to begin with. It was the iron law of the game. One man might have a hundred hard fights in him, another man only twenty; each, according to the make of him and the quality of his fibre[19], had a definite number, and, when he had fought them, he was done. Yes, he had had more fights in him than most of them, and he had had far more than his share of the hard, **gruelling** fights – the kind that worked the heart and lungs to bursting, that took the elastic out of the arteries and made hard knots of muscle out of Youth's sleek suppleness, that **wore out** nerve and **stamina** and made brain and bones weary from excess of effort and endurance overwrought[20]. Yes, he had done better than all of them. There were none of his old fighting partners left. He was the last of the old guard. He had seen them all finished, and he had had a hand in finishing some of them.

They had tried him out against the old uns, and one after another he had put them away – laughing when, like old Stowsher Bill, they cried in the dressing-room. And now he was an old un, and they tried out the youngsters on him. There was that bloke, Sandel. He had come over from New Zealand with a record behind him. But nobody in Australia knew anything about him, so they put him up against old Tom King. If Sandel made a showing[21], he would be given better men to fight, with bigger purses to win; so it was to be depended upon that he would put up a fierce battle. He had everything to win by it – money and glory and career; and Tom King was the grizzled old chopping-block that guarded the highway to fame and fortune[22]. And he had nothing to win except thirty quid, to pay to the landlord and the tradesmen. And, as Tom King thus ruminated, there came to his stolid vision the form of Youth, glorious Youth, rising **exultant** and **invincible**, supple of muscle and silken of skin, with heart and lungs that had never been tired and torn and that laughed at limitation of effort. Yes, Youth was

19 used here to refer to strength, could either be physical or strength of character
20 *unusual*: worked too hard
21 *unusual*: if you make a showing, you give a good performance
22 Tom was the old fighter that younger fighters had to beat to succeed.

the Nemesis[23]. It destroyed the old uns and recked not[24] that, in so doing, it destroyed itself. It enlarged its arteries and smashed its knuckles, and was in turn destroyed by Youth. For Youth was ever youthful. It was only Age that grew old.

At Castlereagh Street he turned to the left, and three blocks along came to the Gayety. A crowd of young larrikins[25] hanging outside the door made respectful way for him, and he heard one say to another: "That's 'im! That's Tom King!"

Inside, on the way to his dressing-room, he encountered the secretary, a keen-eyed, **shrewd-faced** young man, who shook his hand.

"How are you feelin', Tom?" he asked.

"Fit as a fiddle[26]," King answered, though he knew that he lied, and that if he had a quid, he would give it right there for a good piece of steak.

When he emerged from the dressing-room, his seconds behind him, and came down the aisle to the squared ring in the centre of the hall, a burst of greeting and applause went up from the waiting crowd. He acknowledged salutations[27] right and left, though few of the faces did he know. Most of them were the faces of kiddies unborn when he was winning his first **laurels** in the squared ring. He leaped lightly to the raised platform and ducked through the ropes to his corner, where he sat down on a folding stool. Jack Ball, the referee, came over and shook his hand. Ball was a broken-down pugilist who for over ten years had not entered the ring as a principal. King was glad that he had him for referee. They were both old uns. If he should rough it with Sandel a bit beyond the rules, he knew Ball could be depended upon to pass it by.

Aspiring young heavyweights, one after another, were climbing into the ring and being presented to the audience by the referee. Also, he issued their challenges for them.

23 someone or something that opposes you and cannot easily be defeated. The word Nemesis comes from a Greek word meaning 'to give what is owed'.
24 *old-fashioned*: does not realize something or think that it is important
25 *Australian English*: a person who behaves badly in public
26 *informal*: very fit
27 *formal*: a word or phrase that is used for greeting someone

"Young Pronto," Bill announced, "from North Sydney, challenges the winner for fifty pounds side **bet**."

The audience applauded, and applauded again as Sandel himself sprang through the ropes and sat down in his corner. Tom King looked across the ring at him curiously, for in a few minutes they would be locked together in merciless combat, each trying with all the force of him to knock the other into unconsciousness. But little could he see, for Sandel, like himself, had trousers and sweater on over his ring costume. His face was strongly handsome, crowned with a curly mop of yellow hair, while his thick, muscular neck hinted at bodily magnificence.

Young Pronto went to one corner and then the other, shaking hands with the principals and dropping down out of the ring. The challenges went on. Ever Youth climbed through the ropes – Youth unknown, but **insatiable** – crying out to mankind that with strength and skill it would match issues with the winner. A few years before, in his own **heyday** of invincibleness, Tom King would have been amused and bored by these preliminaries. But now he sat fascinated, unable to shake the vision of Youth from his eyes. Always were these youngsters rising up in the boxing game, springing through the ropes and shouting their defiance; and always were the old uns going down before them. They climbed to success over the bodies of the old uns. And ever they came, more and more youngsters – Youth **unquenchable** and irresistible – and ever they put the old uns away, themselves becoming old uns and travelling the same downward path, while behind them, ever pressing on them, was Youth eternal – the new babies, grown lusty and dragging their elders down, with behind them more babies to the end of time – Youth that must have its will and that will never die.

King **glanced** over to the press box and nodded to Morgan, of the *Sportsman*, and Corbett, of the *Referee*. Then he held out his hands, while Sid Sullivan and Charley Bates, his seconds, slipped on his gloves and laced them tight, closely watched by one of Sandel's seconds, who first examined critically the tapes on King's knuckles. A second of his own was in Sandel's corner, performing a like office[28]. Sandel's trousers were pulled off, and, as he stood up, his sweater was skinned off over his head. And Tom King, looking, saw Youth incarnate[29], deep-chested, heavy-thewed[30], with muscles that slipped and slid like live things under the white satin skin. The whole body was a-crawl[31] with life, and Tom King knew that it was a life that had never oozed its freshness out through the aching pores during the long fights wherein Youth paid its **toll** and departed not quite so young as when it entered.

The two men advanced to meet each other, and, as the gong sounded and the seconds clattered out of the ring with the folding stools, they shook hands and instantly took their fighting attitudes. And instantly, like a mechanism of steel and springs balanced **on a hair trigger**, Sandel was in and out and in again, landing a left to the eyes, a right to the ribs, ducking a counter, dancing lightly away and dancing menacingly back again. He was swift and clever. It was a dazzling exhibition. The house yelled its approbation[32]. But King was not dazzled. He had fought too many fights and too many youngsters. He knew the blows for what they were – too quick and too **deft** to be dangerous. Evidently Sandel was going to rush things from the start. It was to be expected. It was the way of Youth, expending its splendour and excellence in wild insurgence and furious onslaught, **overwhelming** opposition with its own unlimited glory of strength and desire.

Sandel was in and out, here, there, and everywhere, light-footed and eager-hearted, a living wonder of white flesh and stinging muscle that **wove** itself into a dazzling fabric of attack, slipping and leaping like a flying shuttle from action to action through a thousand actions, all of them centred upon the destruction of Tom King, who stood between him and fortune. And Tom King patiently endured. He knew his business, and he knew Youth now that Youth was no longer his. There was

28 *formal*: doing a similar job
29 *literary*: in human form
30 *literary*: having big muscles
31 *literary*: crawling
32 *formal*: approval

nothing to do till the other **lost some of his steam**, was his thought, and he **grinned** to himself as he deliberately ducked so as to receive a heavy blow on the top of his head. It was a wicked thing to do, yet eminently fair according to the rules of the boxing game. A man was supposed to take care of his own knuckles, and, if he insisted on hitting an opponent on the top of the head, he did so at his own peril[33]. King could have ducked lower and let the blow whiz harmlessly past, but he remembered his own early fights and how he smashed his first knuckle on the head of the Welsh Terror. He was but playing the game. That duck had accounted for one of Sandel's knuckles. Not that Sandel would mind it now. He would go on, superbly **regardless**, hitting as hard as ever throughout the fight. But later on, when the long ring battles had begun to tell, he would regret that knuckle and look back and remember how he smashed it on Tom King's head.

The first round was all Sandel's, and he had the house yelling with the rapidity of his whirlwind rushes. He overwhelmed King with avalanches of punches, and King did nothing. He never struck once, **contenting himself** with covering up, blocking and ducking and clinching to avoid punishment. He occasionally feinted, shook his head when the weight of a punch landed, and moved stolidly about, never leaping or springing or wasting an ounce of strength. Sandel must foam the froth[34] of Youth away before discreet Age could dare to retaliate. All King's movements were slow and methodical, and his heavy-lidded, slow-moving eyes gave him the appearance of being half asleep or dazed. Yet they were eyes that saw everything, that had been trained to see everything through all his twenty years and odd in the ring. They were eyes that did not blink or **waver** before an impending blow, but that coolly saw and measured distance.

Seated in his corner for the minute's rest at the end of the round, he lay back with outstretched legs, his arms resting on the right angle of the ropes, his chest and abdomen heaving frankly and deeply as he gulped down the air driven by the

33 *literary*: danger
34 King must wait until Sandel's initial energy has died down.

towels of his seconds. He listened with closed eyes to the voices of the house, "Why don't yeh fight, Tom?" many were crying. "Yeh ain't afraid of 'im, are yeh?"

"Muscle-bound," he heard a man on a front seat comment. "He can't move quicker. Two to one[35] on Sandel, in quids."

The gong struck and the two men advanced from their corners. Sandel came forward fully three-quarters of the distance, eager to begin again; but King was content to advance the shorter distance. It was in line with his policy of economy. He had not been well trained, and he had not had enough to eat, and every step counted. Besides, he had already walked two miles to the ringside. It was a repetition of the first round, with Sandel attacking like a whirlwind and with the audience **indignantly** demanding why King did not fight. Beyond feinting and several slowly delivered and ineffectual blows he did nothing save block and stall and clinch. Sandel wanted to make the pace fast, while King, out of his wisdom, refused to accommodate him. He grinned with a certain **wistful pathos** in his ring-battered countenance, and went on **cherishing** his strength with the jealousy of which only Age is capable. Sandel was Youth, and he threw his strength away with the munificent[36] abandon of Youth. To King belonged the ring generalship[37], the wisdom bred of long, aching fights. He watched with cool eyes and head, moving slowly and waiting for Sandel's froth to foam away. To the majority of the onlookers it seemed as though King was hopelessly **outclassed**, and they voiced their opinion in offers of three to one on Sandel. But there were wise ones, a few, who knew King of old time, and who covered what they considered easy money.

The third round began as usual, one-sided, with Sandel doing all the leading, and delivering all the punishment. A half-minute had passed when Sandel, over-confident, left an opening. King's eyes and right arm flashed in the same instant. It was his first real blow – a hook, with the twisted arch of the arm

35 a betting phrase. The speaker is confident that Sandel will win.
36 *formal*: extremely generous
37 the skills or position of an army general

to make it **rigid**, and with all the weight of the half-pivoted body behind it. It was like a sleepy-seeming lion suddenly thrusting out a lightning paw. Sandel, caught on the side of the jaw, was felled like a **bullock**. The audience gasped and murmured **awe-stricken** applause. The man was not muscle-bound, after all, and he could drive a blow like a trip-hammer[38].

Sandel was shaken. He rolled over and attempted to rise, but the sharp yells from his seconds to take the count restrained him. He knelt on one knee, ready to rise, and waited, while the referee stood over him, counting the seconds loudly in his ear. At the ninth he rose in fighting attitude, and Tom King, facing him, knew regret that the blow had not been an inch nearer the point of the jaw. That would have been a knock-out, and he could have carried the thirty quid home to the missus and the kiddies.

The round continued to the end of its three minutes, Sandel for the first time respectful of his opponent and King slow of movement and sleepy-eyed as ever. As the round neared its close, King, warned of the fact by the sight of the seconds **crouching** outside ready for the spring in through the ropes, worked the fight around to his own corner. And when the gong struck, he sat down immediately on the waiting stool, while Sandel had to walk all the way across the diagonal of the square to his own corner. It was a little thing, but it was the sum of little things that counted. Sandel was compelled to walk that many more steps, to give up that much energy, and to lose a part of the precious minute of rest. At the beginning of every round King loafed slowly out from his corner, forcing his opponent to advance the greater distance. The end of every round found the fight manoeuvred by King into his own corner so that he could immediately sit down.

Two more rounds went by, in which King was parsimonious[39] of effort and Sandel prodigal[40]. The latter's[41] attempt to force a

38 a very large, powered hammer used in industry
39 *formal*: not willing to give or spend money
40 *formal*: wasting a lot of money or supplies
41 *formal*: used for referring to the second of two people that have just been mentioned (in this case King)

fast pace made King uncomfortable, for a fair percentage of the multitudinous blows showered upon him went home. Yet King persisted in his **dogged** slowness, despite the crying of the young hot-heads for him to go in and fight. Again, in the sixth round, Sandel was careless, again Tom King's fearful right flashed out to the jaw, and again Sandel took the nine seconds count.

By the seventh round Sandel's pink of condition[42] was gone, and he settled down to what he knew was to be the hardest fight in his experience. Tom King was an old un, but a better old un than he had ever encountered – an old un who never **lost his head**, who was remarkably able at defence, whose blows had the impact of a knotted **club**, and who had a knockout in either hand. Nevertheless, Tom King dared not hit often. He never forgot his battered knuckles, and knew that every hit must count if the knuckles were to last out the fight. As he sat in his corner, glancing across at his opponent, the thought came to him that the sum of his wisdom and Sandel's youth would constitute a world's champion heavyweight. But that was the trouble. Sandel would never become a world champion. He lacked the wisdom, and the only way for him to get it was to buy it with Youth; and when wisdom was his, Youth would have been spent in buying it.

King took every advantage he knew. He never missed an opportunity to clinch, and in effecting most of the clinches his shoulder drove stiffly into the other's ribs. In the philosophy of the ring a shoulder was as good as a punch so far as damage was concerned, and a great deal better so far as concerned expenditure of effort. Also, in the clinches King rested his weight on his opponent, and was loath[43] to let go. This compelled the interference of the referee, who tore them apart, always assisted by Sandel, who had not yet learned to rest. He could not refrain from using those glorious flying arms and **writhing** muscles of his, and when the other rushed into a clinch, striking shoulder against ribs, and with head resting under Sandel's left arm, Sandel almost **invariably** swung his right behind his own back and into

42 *informal old-fashioned*: if you are in the pink of condition, you are healthy and happy
43 *formal*: if you are loath to do something, you are very unwilling to do it

the projecting face. It was a clever stroke, much admired by the audience, but it was not dangerous, and was, therefore, just that much wasted strength. But Sandel was tireless and unaware of limitations, and King grinned and doggedly endured.

Sandel developed a fierce right to the body, which made it appear that King was taking an enormous amount of punishment, and it was only the old ringsters who appreciated the deft touch of King's left glove to the other's biceps just before the impact of the blow. It was true, the blow landed each time; but each time it was robbed of its power by that touch on the biceps. In the ninth round, three times inside a minute, King's right hooked its twisted arch to the jaw; and three times Sandel's body, heavy as it was, was levelled to the mat. Each time he took the nine seconds allowed him and rose to his feet, shaken and **jarred**, but still strong. He had lost much of his speed, and he wasted less effort. He was fighting grimly; but he continued to draw upon his chief asset, which was Youth. King's chief asset was experience. As his vitality had dimmed[44] and his **vigour** abated, he had replaced them with **cunning**, with wisdom born of the long fights and with a careful shepherding[45] of strength. Not alone had he learned never to make a **superfluous** movement, but he had learned how to seduce an opponent into throwing his strength away. Again and again, by feint of foot and hand and body he continued to inveigle[46] Sandel into leaping back, ducking, or countering. King rested, but he never permitted Sandel to rest. It was the strategy of Age.

Early in the tenth round King began stopping the other's rushes with straight lefts to the face, and Sandel, grown **wary**, responded by drawing the left, then by ducking it and delivering his right in a swinging hook to the side of the head. It was too high up to be vitally effective; but when first it landed, King knew the old, familiar descent of the black veil of unconsciousness across his mind. For the instant, or for the slightest fraction of

44 *literary*: become weaker
45 *literary, unusual*: if you shepherd something, you manage and guard it carefully
46 *formal*: persuade someone to do something by using clever or dishonest methods

an instant, rather, he ceased[47]. In the one moment he saw his opponent ducking out of his field of vision and the background of white, watching faces; in the next moment he again saw his opponent and the background of faces. It was as if he had slept for a time and just opened his eyes again, and yet the interval of unconsciousness was so microscopically short that there had been no time for him to fall. The audience saw him totter and his knees give, and then saw him recover and tuck his chin deeper into the shelter of his left shoulder.

Several times Sandel repeated the blow, keeping King partially dazed, and then the latter worked out his defence, which was also a counter. Feinting with his left he took a half-step backward, at the same time upper cutting with the whole strength of his right. So accurately was it timed that it landed squarely on Sandel's face in the full, downward sweep of the duck, and Sandel lifted in the air and curled backward, striking the mat on his head and shoulders. Twice King achieved this, then turned loose and hammered his opponent to the ropes. He gave Sandel no chance to rest or to set himself, but smashed blow in upon blow till the house rose to its feet and the air was filled with an unbroken roar of applause. But Sandel's strength and endurance were superb, and he continued to stay on his feet. A knock-out seemed certain, and a captain of police, **appalled** at the dreadful punishment, arose by the ringside to stop the fight. The gong struck for the end of the round and Sandel staggered to his corner, protesting to the captain that he was sound and strong. To prove it, he threw two back-air-springs, and the police captain gave in.

Tom King, leaning back in his corner and breathing hard, was disappointed. If the fight had been stopped, the referee, perforce[48], would have rendered him the decision and the purse would have been his. Unlike Sandel, he was not fighting for glory or career, but for thirty quid. And now Sandel would **recuperate** in the minute of rest.

47 *formal*: stop happening or continuing
48 *very formal*: in a way that is necessary or that cannot be avoided

Youth will be served – this saying flashed into King's mind, and he remembered the first time he had heard it, the night when he had put away Stowsher Bill. The toff who had bought him a drink after the fight and patted him on the shoulder had used those words. Youth will be served! The toff was right. And on that night in the long ago he had been Youth. To-night Youth sat in the opposite corner. As for himself, he had been fighting for half an hour now, and he was an old man. Had he fought like Sandel, he would not have lasted fifteen minutes. But the point was that he did not recuperate. Those upstanding arteries and that sorely tried heart would not enable him to gather strength in the intervals between the rounds. And he had not had sufficient strength in him to begin with. His legs were heavy under him and beginning to cramp. He should not have walked those two miles to the fight. And there was the steak which he had got up longing for that morning. A great and terrible hatred rose up in him for the butchers who had refused him credit. It was hard for an old man to go into a fight without enough to eat. And a piece of steak was such a little thing, a few pennies at best; yet it meant thirty quid to him.

With the gong that opened the eleventh round, Sandel rushed, making a show of freshness which he did not really possess. King knew it for what it was – a **bluff** as old as the game itself. He clinched to save himself, then, going free, allowed Sandel to get set. This was what King desired. He feinted with his left, drew the answering duck and swinging upward hook, then made the half-step backward, delivered the upper cut full to the face and crumpled Sandel over to the mat. After that he never let him rest, receiving punishment himself, but **inflicting** far more, smashing Sandel to the ropes, hooking and driving all manner of blows into him, tearing away from his clinches or punching him out of attempted clinches, and ever when Sandel would have fallen, catching him with one uplifting hand and with the other immediately smashing him into the ropes where he could not fall.

The house by this time had gone mad, and it was his house, nearly every voice yelling: "Go it, Tom!" "Get 'im! Get 'im!"

"You've got 'im, Tom! You've got 'im!" It was to be a whirlwind finish, and that was what a ringside audience paid to see.

And Tom King, who for half an hour had conserved his strength, now expended it prodigally in the one great effort he knew he had in him. It was his one chance – now or not at all. His strength was **waning** fast, and his hope was that before the last of it **ebbed** out of him he would have beaten his opponent down for the count. And as he continued to strike and force, coolly estimating the weight of his blows and the quality of the damage wrought, he realized how hard a man Sandel was to knock out. Stamina and endurance were his to an extreme degree, and they were the virgin stamina and endurance of Youth. Sandel was certainly a coming[49] man. He had it in him. Only out of such rugged fibre were successful fighters fashioned.

Sandel was reeling and staggering, but Tom King's legs were cramping and his knuckles going back on him. Yet he **steeled himself** to strike the fierce blows, every one of which brought anguish[50] to his tortured hands. Though now he was receiving practically no punishment, he was weakening as rapidly as the other. His blows went home, but there was no longer the weight behind them, and each blow was the result of a severe effort of will. His legs were like **lead**, and they dragged visibly under him; while Sandel's backers, cheered by this symptom, began calling encouragement to their man.

King was **spurred** to a burst of effort. He delivered two blows in succession – a left, a trifle too high, to the solar plexus, and a right cross to the jaw. They were not heavy blows, yet so weak and dazed was Sandel that he went down and lay quivering. The referee stood over him, shouting the count of the fatal seconds in his ear. If before the tenth second was called, he did not rise, the fight was lost. The house stood in hushed silence. King rested on trembling legs. A mortal **dizziness** was upon him, and before his eyes the sea of faces sagged and swayed, while to his ears, as from a remote distance, came the count of the referee.

49 *unusual*: (usually up-and-coming) likely to develop, become successful or become popular soon
50 *formal*: a feeling of great physical or emotional pain

Yet he looked upon the fight as his. It was impossible that a man so punished could rise.

Only Youth could rise, and Sandel rose. At the fourth second he rolled over on his face and **groped** blindly for the ropes. By the seventh second he had dragged himself to his knee, where he rested, his head rolling **groggily** on his shoulders. As the referee cried "Nine!" Sandel stood upright, in proper stalling position, his left arm wrapped about his face, his right wrapped about his stomach. Thus were his vital points guarded, while he lurched forward toward King in the hope of effecting a clinch and gaining more time.

At the instant Sandel arose, King was at him, but the two blows he delivered were **muffled** on the stalled arms. The next moment Sandel was in the clinch and holding on desperately while the referee **strove** to drag the two men apart. King helped to force himself free. He knew the rapidity with which Youth recovered, and he knew that Sandel was his if he could prevent that recovery. One stiff punch would do it. Sandel was his, **indubitably** his. He had out-generalled him, out-fought him, out-pointed[51] him. Sandel reeled out of the clinch, balanced on the hair line between defeat or survival. One good blow would topple him over and down and out. And Tom King, in a flash of **bitterness**, remembered the piece of steak and wished that he had it then behind that necessary punch he must deliver. He nerved himself for the blow, but it was not heavy enough nor swift enough. Sandel swayed, but did not fall, staggering back to the ropes and holding on. King staggered after him, and, with a **pang** like that of dissolution[52], delivered another blow. But his body had **deserted** him. All that was left of him was a fighting intelligence that was dimmed and clouded from exhaustion. The blow that was aimed for the jaw struck no higher than the shoulder. He had willed the blow higher, but the tired muscles had not been able to obey. And, from the impact of the blow, Tom King himself reeled back and nearly fell. Once again he strove. This time his punch missed altogether, and, from

51 *out-* prefix: bigger, better, longer etc: used with many verbs; here with more points
52 *formal*: the process of gradually getting weaker or smaller and then disappearing

absolute weakness, he fell against Sandel and clinched, holding on to him to save himself from sinking to the floor.

King did not attempt to free himself. He had shot his bolt[53]. He was gone. And Youth had been served. Even in the clinch he could feel Sandel growing stronger against him. When the referee thrust them apart, there, before his eyes, he saw Youth recuperate. From instant to instant Sandel grew stronger. His punches, weak and futile at first, became stiff and accurate. Tom King's bleared eyes saw the gloved fist driving at his jaw, and he willed to guard it by interposing his arm. He saw the danger, willed the act; but the arm was too heavy. It seemed burdened with a hundredweight of lead. It would not lift itself, and he strove to lift it with his soul. Then the gloved fist landed home. He experienced a sharp snap that was like an electric spark, and, simultaneously, the veil of blackness enveloped him.

When he opened his eyes again he was in his corner, and he heard the yelling of the audience like the roar of the surf at Bondi Beach[54]. A wet sponge was being pressed against the base of his brain, and Sid Sullivan was blowing cold water in a refreshing spray over his face and chest. His gloves had already been removed, and Sandel, bending over him, was shaking his hand. He bore no ill-will toward the man who had put him out and he returned the grip with a heartiness that made his battered knuckles protest. Then Sandel stepped to the centre of the ring and the audience hushed its **pandemonium** to hear him accept young Pronto's challenge and offer to increase the side bet to one hundred pounds. King looked on **apathetically** while his seconds mopped the streaming water from him, dried his face, and prepared him to leave the ring. He felt hungry. It was not the ordinary, **gnawing** kind, but a great faintness, a palpitation at the pit of the stomach that communicated itself to all his body. He remembered back into the fight to the moment when he had Sandel swaying and tottering on the hair-line balance of defeat. Ah, that piece of steak would have done it! He had

53 *informal*: use all your resources or energy in doing something
54 a famous beach in Sydney

lacked just that for the decisive blow, and he had lost. It was all because of the piece of steak.

His seconds were half-supporting him as they helped him through the ropes. He tore free from them, ducked through the ropes unaided, and leaped heavily to the floor, following on their heels as they forced a passage for him down the crowded centre aisle. Leaving the dressing-room for the street, in the entrance to the hall, some young fellow spoke to him.

"W'y didn't yuh go in an' get 'im when yuh 'ad 'im?" the young fellow asked.

"Aw, go to hell!" said Tom King, and passed down the steps to the sidewalk.

The doors of the public-house[55] at the corner were swinging wide, and he saw the lights and the smiling barmaids, heard the many voices discussing the fight and the prosperous chink of money on the bar. Somebody called to him to have a drink. He hesitated perceptibly, then refused and went on his way.

He had not a copper in his pocket, and the two-mile walk home seemed very long. He was certainly getting old. Crossing the Domain, he sat down suddenly on a bench, unnerved by the thought of the missus sitting up for him, waiting to learn the outcome of the fight. That was harder than any knockout, and it seemed almost impossible to face.

He felt weak and sore, and the pain of his smashed knuckles warned him that, even if he could find a job at navvy work, it would be a week before he could grip a **pick** handle or a **shovel**. The hunger palpitation at the pit of the stomach was sickening. His **wretchedness** overwhelmed him, and into his eyes came an unwonted[56] moisture. He covered his face with his hands, and, as he cried, he remembered Stowsher Bill and how he had served him that night in the long ago. Poor old Stowsher Bill! He could understand now why Bill had cried in the dressing-room.

55 *formal*: a pub
56 *formal*: not usual for a particular person or thing and therefore unexpected

Post-reading activities

Understanding the story

Use these questions to help you check that you have understood the story.

At home

1 How many people are there in the King house? Who are they?
2 How many of them eat supper? Why?
3 In what ways does King look like a typical boxer?
4 Does his appearance fit with his character? Why/Why not?
5 What is King's attitude to his opponents in the ring?
6 What are the long-term effects of boxing on his body?
7 Why was Lizzie unable to get steak for his supper? What did the butchers refuse to do? Why?
8 What training has King done for his fight? What training could he have done to be better prepared?
9 'He should have had better food and no worries.' What do you think is worrying him? Why do you think that worry had a negative effect on his preparation?
10 Where has King got money from recently?
11 How is Lizzie's behaviour different before this fight?
12 Why will he receive nothing if he loses?
13 How does his journey to the fight compare with previous journeys to fights when he was younger?
14 What regrets does King have?
15 Why is Stowsher Bill significant for King? How does he feel towards him now?
16 Is King's career typical of the majority of boxers? Why/Why not?
17 Why have the organizers arranged a match between King and Sandel?

Before the fight

18 Why is King happy with the referee?
19 What is King's initial impression of Sandel?
20 Summarize in one sentence King's 'vision of Youth'.
21 Why is one of Sandel's seconds in King's corner?

The fight

22 Who seems to be winning after the first round?
23 What does King do that he thinks will cause Sandel problems later in the match?
24 What happens in round three that surprises the audience?
25 Why is King not happy with this?
26 How do the next three rounds mirror the first three?
27 What different ways does King use to conserve his energy?
28 Which of the following rounds are King's? Which are Sandel's?
    1, 2, 3, 4, 5, 6, 9, 10
29 Why does the police captain want to stop the fight after round ten? Why doesn't he stop it? How does King feel about this?
30 What is Sandel's big advantage at this late stage in the fight?
31 Why does King suddenly think of steak at this moment?
32 How many times does each fighter fall to the ground in round eleven?
33 What does King do after the fight?

Language study

Grammar

The past perfect

A *Piece of Steak* is written chronologically, which is to say the events of the story are recounted in time order, from start to finish. However, it frequently refers to events that happened earlier, often years ago in Tom King's career, when he was a young boxer. To do this, the past perfect is used.

Form

The structure is formed: *had* + past participle. It exists in simple and continuous forms, and can be in the active or passive voice:

*He **had done** a few days' navvy work when he could get it (past perfect simple)*

*The knuckles, smashed and battered, testified to the use to which they **had been put**. (passive)*

*He realized that it was the old uns he **had been putting away**. (continuous)*

1 Read the first paragraph again. How many instances of the past perfect are there? Are there any in the passive voice? Are there any instances of the past perfect continuous?

Use

We use the past perfect simple to say that an action finished before a certain point in the past:

*On that night in the long ago he **had been** Youth. Tonight Youth **sat** in the opposite corner.*

The continuous form of the past perfect is used to emphasize that the action was in progress for some time before a point in the past or to emphasize the duration of the action:

*He **had been fighting** for half an hour now.*

The past perfect can be used just once to establish a return to a previous time; other actions in that period can be described using the past simple:

*He **had not had** a fair training for this fight. It was a drought year in Australia, times were hard, and even the most irregular work **was** difficult to find. He **had** no sparring partner, and his food **was** not of the best nor always sufficient. He **did** a few days' navvy work when he could get it, and he **ran** around the Domain in the early mornings to get his legs in shape.*

2 Compare the passage above with the original version on page 93. Are they the same? What does the writer do instead?

3 Here are some of the events of the story in chronological order. Rewrite them in two ways, versions a) and b), starting with event 5. Use the past perfect:

a) once to establish the return to a previous time period
b) consistently throughout that period, like the writer of the story.

1 King left the club on his own.
2 He was invited for a drink but refused it.
3 He was walking through the Domain when he sat down on a bench and cried.
4 After a while, he slowly stood up and dragged himself home.
5 He stopped at his front door. He had absolutely nothing left, except Lizzie, his wife, and the kiddies. What was he going to tell them?

   King stopped …

4 Compare your two versions. Which do you prefer? Why?

Expressing regret

King very nearly wins the fight. He is aware of things that affected the outcome, and looking back, feels sorry that they were not different.

5 Underline the key structures that express regret in the following sentences and answer the questions.

1 He _should not have walked_ those two miles to the fight.
2 He found himself wishing that he had learned a trade. It would have been better in the long run.
3 Sandel would regret having smashed that knuckle on Tom King's head.
4 Tom King knew regret that the blow had not been an inch nearer the jaw. If he had, it would have been a knock-out, and he could have carried the thirty quid home to the missus and the kiddies.

a) What <u>three</u> modal verbs can be used to express regret? (modal + *have* + past participle)
b) Which of these sentences with regret is **not** grammatically correct?
   i) Tom regretted that he had not eaten steak.
   ii) Tom regretted not to have eaten steak.
   iii) Tom regretted not having eaten steak.
c) What verb structure goes after *wish* to express regret?
d) Which conditional structure is used to express regret?

6 Rewrite this series of unfortunate events as regrets using structures from 5 above.

King did not find much navvy work. They didn't have enough money to buy food. Lizzie could not buy her husband any meat. King didn't have any steak for dinner. He didn't have enough strength to knock Sandel out. He lost. He didn't win the thirty pounds winner's purse. The family couldn't pay back the tradesmen ...

   King wished ...

Vocabulary

Collocations: quantifiers

The story title, *A Piece of Steak* contains a quantifier, a word or phrase that is used with another word to show how much of it there is. Steak could also be quantified with other words, such as *a lot of*, *a cut of* or *not enough*. Other quantifiers appear in the story.

7 Match the quantifiers (1–13) to a collocating noun (a–m).

1	a burst of	a)	a second
2	a crowd of	b)	bread
3	a fraction of	c)	blows
4	a mop of	d)	effort
5	a morsel of	e)	service
6	a shower of	f)	yellow hair
7	long years of	g)	people
8	a hint of	h)	applause
9	a lump of	i)	desperation
10	a period of	j)	faces
11	a roar of	k)	money
12	a sea of	l)	rest
13	an ounce of	m)	strength

8 Use collocations from 7 to complete the sentences.

1 After an initial .... of ...., he lost interest in his job.

2 At the end of the concert there was .... of
....

3 He called her at midnight. There was .... of
.... in his voice.

4 He didn't have .... of .... left to carry any more boxes.

5 How strange! For .... of .... then, I thought I saw Philip.

6 The company gave her nothing, despite all her .... of
....

7 You need a holiday. .... of .... will do you so much good.

8 Arriving at the office, there was .... of .... waiting for her.

Compound adjectives

The story contains a great deal of description. In order to create adjectives with very specific meanings, the writer uses compound adjectives – adjectives formed by more than one word.

9 Which compound adjectives describe King? Which describe Sandel? Can you remember who the others describe?

1 keen-eyed	7 ring-battered
2 heavy-lidded	8 awe-stricken
3 shrewd-faced	9 villainous-looking
4 eager-hearted	10 sleepy-seeming
5 deep-chested	11 slow-moving
6 light-footed	12 lion-like

There may be many possible combinations; as well as keen-eyed, other words such as blue-eyed, eagle-eyed and wide-eyed are also possible. These common combinations act as independent words and can be found in good dictionaries. However, it is also possible to create new compounds by following certain rules.

Form

There are a variety of ways of making compound adjectives. Here are three:

1 Add the past participle to an adjective or adverb when the thing or person being described is not the subject of the past participle:

   an old-fashioned car, dimly-lit streets

2 Add the present participle to an adjective, adverb or noun when the thing or person described is the subject:

   a never-ending story, a slow-growing plant, a good-looking woman

3 Some use other words with special meanings:

   flu-like symptoms (-like = similar to)
   a hands-free phone (-free = without)
   a forty-mile journey

10 Rewrite these phrases using compound adjectives.

1 a baseball player who hits hard
   a hard-hitting baseball player

2 a boy who someone bruised badly

3 a building that looks similar to a ship

4 a hot drink that tastes sweet

5 a sport that is growing fast

6 a painting that people forgot about for a long time

7 a wine that looks expensive

8 a city that is populated densely

9 skin cream that has no fragrance

10 tomatoes that are dried in the sun

Literary analysis

Plot

1 Before the fight we learn some important information about the two
  boxers. Put the information in the order that we learn it:
  a) Lizzie's attempt to buy some steak
  b) how much money King makes from the fight
  c) King's character
  d) King's appearance
  e) Sandel's appearance
  f) what King has for dinner
  g) King's successful career as a younger boxer
  h) King's preparation for the fight

2 During the fight, the chance of King winning seems to rise and fall
  as the fight progresses. After each round, measure how optimistic
  you feel about King winning:
  a) *I think King will win*
  b) *Either boxer could win*
  c) *I think Sandel will win*

3 What options for making money does King have now, if any? What
  would you do if you were King?

4 A 'vicious circle' is a process in which the existence of a problem causes other problems, and this makes the original problem worse. In what sense is poverty a vicious circle, according to the story?

5 Imagine King had won the fight. Would that change the message of the story?

6 Do you think this is a story for men rather than women? Why/Why not?

7 In your opinion, does the story glorify boxing?

8 What was your attitude to the sport of boxing before you read the story? Has your attitude changed at all? If so, why?

The role of food in the story

9 What does the food in the story tell us about the King family?

10 Why does the narrator explain that King had given his dog steak when he was successful?

11 Why would a piece of steak have helped King?

12 Tom's meal happens at the very start of the story. When is steak mentioned during the fight? Why at those points?

13 Why is the story called *A Piece of Steak*?

14 The word *steak* sounds identical to another word, *stake*, which is used in the story. It means the things that you can lose by taking a risk. Do you think this is a coincidence? Why/Why not?

Character

15 Read paragraphs 2 and 3 of the story again (pages 90–91). What impression of King do you get from this? How sympathetic are you to his character?

16 Now read the next two paragraphs. Has your impression of King changed at all? In what way?

17 Do you think there is any significance in Tom's surname?

18 Here is the first description of Sandel:

His face was strongly handsome, crowned with a curly mop of yellow hair, while his thick, muscular neck hinted at bodily magnificence.

What image or comparisons do the words 'crowned' and 'magnificence' convey?

19 Allegory is a literary device defined as 'the use of events and characters as symbols'. What do the two fighters symbolize? To what extent is King simply a symbol? Is there more to his character than this? What about Sandel? Is he just an allegory?

Narration

20 How much of the story is taken up describing each round? Why are some rounds given more attention than others?

21 The narrator tells the story from King's point of view. How does King's interpretation of events affect the telling of the story? How would the story have been different if it had been told from Sandel's point of view?

22 We are told that 'Tom King had never been a talker'. Even though he says very little, we sometimes hear his 'voice'. Read extracts a) and b): which sounds like King speaking? Which the narrator? How do you know?

   a) *Tom King knew that it was a life that had never oozed its freshness out through the aching pores during the long fights wherein Youth paid its toll and departed not quite so young as when it entered.*

   b) *He remembered the time he put out old Stowsher Bill, at Rush-Cutters Bay, in the eighteenth round, and how old Bill had cried afterward in the dressing-room like a baby. Perhaps old Bill's rent had been overdue. Perhaps he'd had at home a missus an' a couple of kiddies.*

23 The description of the fight is long but it never gets boring. If you made a film of this story, how would you direct it? Think about the length of shots and special effects such as slow motion or freeze frame.

Style

24 The following sentence describes the time in King's career when he was a champion. How many noun phrases are there? Are there any verbs? What is the effect of this sentence?
Big money – sharp, glorious fights – periods of rest and loafing in between – a following of eager flatterers, the slaps on the back, the shakes of the hand, the toffs glad to buy him a drink for the privilege of five minutes' talk – and the glory of it, the yelling houses, the whirlwind finish, the referee's "King wins!" and his name in the sporting columns next day.

25 Read the paragraph describing King's vision of Youth (page 98, starting: 'Young Pronto went to one corner …'). Notice the repetition of many of the words throughout the paragraph. Which words and ideas are repeated? What is the effect of this? How does this effect mirror the vision he has?

26 In the following sentence, what structure is repeated? What is the effect?

After that he never let him rest, receiving punishment himself, but inflicting far more, smashing Sandel to the ropes, hooking and driving all manner of blows into him, tearing away from his clinches or punching him out of attempted clinches, and ever when Sandel would have fallen, catching him with one uplifting hand and with the other immediately smashing him into the ropes where he could not fall.

27 Read the account of the eleventh round again, starting on page 106 ('With the gong …'). How does the narrator keep us guessing about who the winner will be?

28 What is the final image of Tom that we are left with? How does it make you feel about Tom?

Guidance to the above literary terms, answer keys to all the exercises and activities, plus a wealth of other reading-practice material, can be found at: www.macmillanenglish.com/readers.

Like Water for Chocolate: January

by Laura Esquivel

About the author

Laura Esquivel is a Mexican author and screenwriter for television and cinema. She is an important figure in Mexican cultural life, but is still best known as the author of *Like Water for Chocolate*, which she wrote in 1989.

Esquivel was born in 1950 in Mexico City, the third of four children. The kitchen was central to her childhood, and her mother and grandmother taught her a love of the magic of cooking and Mexican cooking traditions. It was in the kitchen that she heard family stories and learnt family traditions. The first inspiration for her famous novel can be found here; she heard about an aunt, called Tita, who could not get married because she had to look after her mother.

Theatre has always been a part of her life – she remembers her father used an old tape recorder to record stories and plays that the children used to perform. Her first job was as a nursery school teacher; she used to write stories and plays for her pupils to act out. This quickly developed, and while still a young teacher, she helped to start the Theatre and Literature Workshop for Children. She was then asked to write television programmes for children for the national cultural channel. Before she was thirty years old she had begun her career in television.

She met and married film director Alfonso Aráu and he encouraged her to write for the cinema. In 1985 her first screenplay, *Chido Guan, el Tacos de Oro*, written with her husband, was made into a film. Nevertheless, she was frustrated by filmmaking, which she felt limited her ideas. Although she had written several screenplays by herself, none of them had been turned into films. Her answer was to write a novel instead. She says that *Like Water for Chocolate* 'was a way to make my ideal film, one that no one else would make'.

When the novel was published, it became an immediate success in the Spanish-speaking world, and was soon translated into English and more than thirty other languages. Not only that, but it *was* made into a film, directed again by Aráu. It is difficult for foreign-language films to do well in the English-speaking world, but *Like Water for Chocolate* quickly became one of the most popular subtitled films in the USA and is still in the top ten foreign-language films of all time.

The novel and the film changed Esquivel's life. She and Aráu got divorced after they argued about the legal rights to the screenplay. Since then she has continued to write successful novels, and plays an important role in Mexican cultural life, recently entering politics.

When Esquivel became famous in the 1990s, greater attention was being paid to voices in literature that had not been listened to previously, such as those of writers from ethnic minorities and women. There was great interest in multicultural themes and writers. Esquivel's writing provided fresh expression of feminist themes and issues surrounding Latin American identity. For these reasons, as well as her creativity and storytelling skills, she is seen as an important contributor to world literature.

About the story

Like Water for Chocolate was published in 1989 and translated into English in 1992. The title is a local expression; in Mexico, hot chocolate is made with water instead of milk. Chocolate pieces are dropped into water only when it is boiling. If you are 'like water for chocolate', you are extremely hot, which might mean that you are very angry or very passionate.

The full title of the story is *Like Water for Chocolate: A Novel in Monthly Installments with Recipes, Romances and Home Remedies*. The extract that you are going to read, 'January', is the first chapter of the book, and as the title suggests, each chapter contains a recipe as well as a story about love.

Background information

Food in the story

Each chapter in *Like Water for Chocolate* begins with a list of ingredients for a traditional Mexican dish. The recipe that introduces Chapter One, Christmas rolls, includes two key ingredients in Mexican cooking: chorizo sausage and *chile serrano*.

Chile, or chilli as it is spelt in English, is an ingredient found in most savoury meals in Mexican cooking. It is a green or red vegetable that is usually small and thin in shape, which has a strong, spicy flavour. The strength, or 'heat' of the flavour depends on the particular type of chilli, and the way it is prepared and cooked. Some chillies are not much hotter than a green pepper, while others, such as the *serrano* variety used here, are extremely hot – too spicy for many people.

Chorizo is a sausage that contains strong flavours, too. Originating in Spain and Portugal, chorizo was introduced to Mexico by the early Europeans, but rather than use paprika to flavour the meat, in Mexico dried chilli powder is used instead. Mexicans tend to eat their sausage broken up in small pieces rather than in large slices.

Mexican food typically includes the ingredients described above, along with *tortilla*, a type of thin bread made from maize flour, rolled or folded and filled with cheese, beans or meat. Examples of this are *enchiladas* (rolled) and *tacos* (folded and cooked).

The ingredients and the procedure for making Christmas rolls are explained in the extract but there is a short version of the recipe on page 191.

Traditional male and female roles

Traditionally, Latin American culture was influenced by the idea of *machismo*, an intense form of masculine behaviour. Men in Mexico were expected to be authoritarian and aggressive, while women had to be submissive and dependent on men for many things. A woman's life was determined by the man she married; both before and after marriage, she had little control over important life decisions. Arranged marriages were common, in which parents decided who a woman would marry. It was not unusual to prevent a daughter from marrying so that she would stay at home and look after her elderly parents. One area where women could make decisions was in domestic matters: arranging social events and cooking, for example.

Summary

It may help you to know something about what happens in the story before you read it. Don't worry, this summary does not tell you how the story ends!

The novel is set in Mexico in the early years of the twentieth century. Tita is the youngest of three sisters in the De la Garza family. They live with their mother Elena, the cook, Nacha and the maid, Chencha, on a ranch – a Mexican farm. The extract you are going to read, Chapter One of the book, starts by describing Tita's dramatic birth on the table in the kitchen.

Her father dies when she is just two days old, and her mother is so upset that she stops producing milk for her baby. Nacha offers to feed Tita with food from the kitchen, so Tita spends most of her childhood around Nacha and her work. The kitchen becomes her whole world. One day she invites her older sisters to play a game in the kitchen. Rosaura, the second daughter, burns her hands on the hot cooker. After that, her mother does not let her play with her sisters, so she only has Nacha to play with.

The women are making sausages all together one day when Tita, who is almost sixteen years old, nervously tells her mother to expect a visit from a young man, Pedro Muzquiz. Pedro wants to ask her whether he can marry Tita, but Mama Elena tells Tita that she will never get married because, as the youngest daughter, her duty is to stay with her mother and look after her in her old age.

Tita is understandably very angry, but she doesn't feel she can argue against her mother's wishes, so she sends word to Pedro not to come to the house. Inexplicably, he never receives the message, and arrives to speak to Elena. The decision that is made in that meeting between Tita's mother and the man she loves will affect her life for ever.

Pre-reading activities

Key vocabulary

This section will help you familiarize yourself with some of the more specific vocabulary used in the extract. You may want to use it to help you before you start reading, or as a revision exercise after you have finished the story.

Food-related words

1 **Look at the extracts below, then match the words (1–13) with their definitions (a–m).**

*Hard **rolls** can easily be obtained from a bakery.*

*Add the **sardines**, which have been **deboned**.*

*Tita made her entrance into this world amid the smells of **simmering** noodle soup.*

*She grew healthy on a diet of teas and thin corn **gruels**.*

*The girls watched the dancing water drops dribbled on a red-hot **griddle**.*

*The water was ready for **plucking** the chickens.*

*She had been walking to the table carrying a tray of **egg-yolk** candies.*

*She understood how **dough** feels when it is plunged into boiling oil.*

*She was afraid she would start to bubble like **batter**.*

*They are **steeped** in hot water for fifteen days. Then the spirit is **distilled**. Four ounces of orange-flower water are added, and the mixture is stirred and **strained**.*

1 batter	6 griddle	11 steep
2 roll	7 gruel	12 strain
3 debone	8 pluck	13 yolk
4 distil	9 sardines	
5 dough	10 simmer	

a) a food made by boiling crushed grain in water or milk, often eaten by poor people in the past
b) a flat iron pan used on top of a hot surface for cooking
c) the middle part of an egg that is yellow
d) a mixture of flour, fat and water that is baked to make bread or pastry

e) pull the feathers off the body of a dead bird so that it can be cooked
f) a liquid mixture of milk, flour and eggs, used in cooking
g) make a liquid more pure by heating it until it becomes a gas and then making it colder so that it becomes a liquid again
h) separate a solid from a liquid by pouring it into a bowl with a lot of small holes in it
i) leave food in a liquid for some time
j) cook slowly at a temperature near boiling
k) a silver fish used for food, either cooked and eaten fresh or preserved in tins (= metal containers. In US English *tins* are called *cans*)
l) remove the bones from meat or fish before cooking it
m) bread in the form of a small round or long shape

Herbs

2 **Herbs are plants used for adding flavour to food. What are the following herbs called in your language? Use a bilingual dictionary to help you.**

oregano   bay leaves   coriander   thyme

Clothes and sewing

3 **Read the extracts and decide whether the words in bold are a), b) or c).**

a) things made of fabric, e.g. items of clothing
b) items needed for making clothes
c) techniques for making clothes or elements in those techniques

*There would be no ironing, no **embroidery,** no sewing that day.*

*Mama Elena, who was inspecting the clothes each of the women had been sewing, discovered that Tita's creation, which was the most perfect, had not been **basted** before it was sewed. 'Congratulations,' she said, 'your **stitches** are perfect – but you didn't baste it, did you?'*

*She had to get rid of that cold. First she put on a wool **robe** and a heavy **cloak**. Then she put on felt **slippers** and another two **shawls**. Finally she went to her **sewing box** and pulled out the **bedspread** she had started the day Pedro first spoke of marriage. A bedspread like that, a **crocheted** one, takes about a year to complete. She decided to use the **yarn**, not to let it go to waste.*

4 Check your answers in 3 with the definitions in the box below.

yarn cotton, wool or other fibres in the form of thick thread (= a substance like string)

stitch a short piece of thread that you can see on cloth when it has been sewn

slippers soft comfortable shoes that you wear in your house

shawl a large piece of material that is worn by a woman around her shoulders or on her head

sewing box a container for keeping equipment and cloth for making clothes and other items

robe a piece of clothing like a long loose coat that you wear in your house

embroidery the activity of decorating cloth with coloured stitches

crochet make a piece of cloth that has a pattern of holes, using wool or cotton thread and a large needle with a hook on the end

cloak a long, loose coat without sleeves, that fastens around your neck

bedspread a top cover for a bed, used mainly for decoration

baste sew cloth together with long loose stitches, often called tacking, that will hold them while you finish sewing it with permanent stitches (in *An Old-Fashioned Thanksgiving*, *baste* has a different meaning)

Words associated with crying

5 Read the words and definitions in the box, then choose the best word to complete the sentences below.

whimper make small sounds of pain, fear or sadness

well up if a liquid wells or wells up, it comes to the surface and is about to flow out

weep *literary*: cry

wail shout or cry with a long, high sound

sobs loud noises made when crying

shed tears produce tears

drown out prevent a sound from being heard by making a louder noise

1 Her *tears/sobs* were so loud that even the next-door neighbours could hear them.

2 She needed to *weep/whimper* for the loss of her husband.

3 The baby *wailed/welled up* most of the night.

4 The crying almost *drowned out/welled up* the sound of his voice.

5 The dog licked its leg; its quiet *whimpering/wailing* sounded pitiful.

6 With tears *welling up/shedding* in his eyes, Palmer walked away.

7 We won't be *drowning out/shedding* any tears when he leaves. He isn't a very popular boss!

Exercising authority and responding to it

There are moments in the story when Elena, the only parent in the De la Garza household, exercises her authority over her daughters. The daughters are expected to do as she says.

6 Read the verbs and definitions in the box. Which do you associate with a) a person in authority b) a person under someone else's authority?

deny *formal:* not allow someone to have something
endure suffer something difficult or unpleasant in a patient way over a long period
forbid tell someone that they must not do something
obey do what a law or a person says that you must do
permit allow someone to do something
protest disagree strongly with something, often by making a formal statement or taking action in public
rebel oppose orders or traditions, or do things in ways that are not what people expect you to do
repress use force or violence to control people
resist fight against someone or something
subdue stop someone from behaving in an uncontrolled or violent way
submit *formal:* agree to obey a rule, a law or a decision

Phrasal verbs

7 Read the phrasal verbs and definitions in the box, then choose an appropriate verb in the correct form to complete the sentences below.

bow before (usually **bow to**) agree to do what someone wants you to do, although you do not want to
bring something on be the cause of something bad, especially an illness
dish up put food into dishes or on plates so that it is ready to be eaten
fill someone in *informal* give someone details about something
fly by if time flies by, it seems to pass very quickly
keep up continue to do something
pass for be accepted, wrongly, as being a particular type of thing
be wrapped up in be involved in something completely

1 She nearly died of a heart attack .... by fear.
2 Did Sam .... you .... about the new project?
3 They were .... in criminal activities.
4 Six months ...., and it was time to come home again.
5 They finally .... political pressure and signed the agreement.

6 Can you wash your hands? I'm about to .... dinner.

7 I can't stand the name-calling that .... political debate these days.

8 Well done, Amam, if you .... this good work you could win the top student award!

Main themes

Before you read the extract, you may want to think about some of its main themes. The questions will help you think about the extract as you are reading it for the first time. There is more discussion of the main themes in the *Literary analysis* section after the extract.

Parental authority

In most families there are rules and traditions which family members are expected to respect. The children may wish to follow these rules or fight against them.

8 As you read the extract, ask yourself the following questions:

a) Is Elena's authority generally respected in her house?

b) How do her daughters show their respect, or otherwise, for her authority?

c) To what extent are Tita and her sisters free to choose their own fate (what will happen to them)?

Expressing emotion

Emotions are important in the story. Sometimes these feelings are hidden, sometimes they are expressed normally and sometimes they show themselves in unusual ways.

9 Think about these questions while you read:

a) What emotions are felt by the different characters?

b) When do characters try to hide their emotions in the story? When do they express them?

c) How are these emotions expressed?

Like Water for Chocolate: January

by Laura Esquivel

Christmas Rolls

INGREDIENTS
1 can of sardines
½ chorizo sausage
1 onion
oregano
1 can of chiles serranos
10 hard rolls

PREPARATION:
Take care to chop the onion fine. To keep from crying when
you chop it (which is so annoying!), I suggest you place a little
bit on your head. The trouble with crying over an onion is that
once the chopping gets you started and the tears begin to well
up, the next thing you know you just can't stop. I don't know
whether that's ever happened to you, but I have to confess it's
happened to me, many times. Mama used to say it was because I
was especially sensitive to onions, like my great-aunt, Tita.

Tita was so sensitive to onions, any time they were being
chopped, they say she would just cry and cry; when she was
still in my great-grandmother's belly her sobs were so loud that
even Nacha, the cook, who was half-deaf, could hear them
easily. Once her wailing got so violent that it brought on an
early **labour**. And before my great-grandmother could let out a
word or even a whimper, Tita made her entrance into this world,
prematurely, right there on the kitchen table amid[1] the smells
of simmering noodle soup, thyme, bay leaves and coriander,
steamed milk, garlic and, of course, onion. Tita had no need
of the usual **slap** on the bottom, because she was already crying

1 *literary:* surrounded by things or people

as she emerged; maybe that was because she knew then that it would be her **lot in life** to be denied marriage. The way Nacha tells it, Tita was literally washed into this world on a great tide[2] of tears that spilled over the edge of the table and flooded across the kitchen floor.

That afternoon, when the **uproar** had subsided and the water had been dried up by the sun, Nacha swept up the residue the tears had left on the red stone floor. There was enough salt to fill a ten-pound[3] sack – it was used for cooking and lasted a long time. Thanks to her unusual birth, Tita felt a deep love for the kitchen, where she spent most of her life from the day she was born.

When she was only two days old, Tita's father, my great-grandfather, died of a heart attack and Mama Elena's milk dried up from the shock. Since there was no such thing as powdered milk in those days, and they couldn't find a wet nurse[4] anywhere, they were in a panic to satisfy the infant's hunger. Nacha, who knew everything about cooking – and much more that doesn't enter the picture until later – offered to take charge of feeding Tita. She felt she had the best chance of 'educating the innocent child's stomach', even though she had never married or had children. Though she didn't know how to read or write, when it came to cooking she knew everything there was to know. Mama Elena accepted her offer gratefully; she had enough to do between her **mourning** and the enormous responsibility of running the ranch – and it was the ranch that would provide her children with the food and education they deserved – without having to worry about feeding a newborn baby on top of everything else.

From that day on, Tita's **domain** was the kitchen, where she grew **vigorous** and healthy on a diet of teas and thin corn gruels. This explains the sixth sense Tita developed about everything concerning food. Her eating habits, for example, were **attuned** to the kitchen routine: in the morning, when she could smell

2 *literary*: a large, unstoppable movement of water
3 one pound is 454 grammes. There are 16 ounces in a pound.
4 *old-fashioned*: a woman who is paid to feed another woman's baby with her own breast milk

that the beans were ready; at midday, when she sensed the water was ready for plucking the chickens; and in the afternoon, when the dinner bread was baking, Tita knew it was time for her to be fed.

Sometimes she would cry for no reason at all, like when Nacha chopped onions, but since they both knew the cause of these tears, they didn't pay them much mind. They made them a source of entertainment, so that during her childhood Tita didn't distinguish between tears of laughter and tears of sorrow. For her laughing was a form of crying.

Likewise for Tita the joy of living was wrapped up in the delights of food. It wasn't easy for a person whose knowledge of life was based on the kitchen to comprehend the outside world. That world was an endless **expanse** that began at the door between the kitchen and the rest of the house, whereas everything on the kitchen side of that door, on through the door leading to the patio and the kitchen and herb gardens was completely hers – it was Tita's realm[5].

Her sisters were just the opposite: to them, Tita's world seemed full of unknown dangers, and they were terrified of it. They felt that playing in the kitchen was foolish and dangerous. But once Tita managed to convince them to join her in watching the dazzling display made by dancing water drops **dribbled** on a red-hot griddle.

While Tita was singing and waving her wet hands in time, showering drops of water down on the griddle so they would dance, Rosaura was **cowering** in the corner, **stunned** by the display. Gertrudis, on the other hand, found this game enticing, and she threw herself into it with the enthusiasm she always showed where rhythm, movement or music were involved. Then Rosaura had tried to join them – but since she barely **moistened** her hands and then shook them **gingerly**, her efforts didn't have the desired effect, so Tita tried to move her hands closer to the griddle. Rosaura resisted, and they struggled for control until Tita became annoyed and let go, but that momentum carried Rosaura's hands on to it. Tita got a terrible **spanking** for that,

5 *mainly literary*: a country ruled by a king or queen

and she was forbidden to play with her sisters in her own world. Nacha became her playmate then. Together they made up all sorts of games and activities to do with cooking. Like the day they saw a man in the village plaza[6] twisting long thin balloons into animal shapes, and they decided to do the same with sausages. They didn't just make real animals, they also made up some of their own, creatures with the neck of a swan, the legs of a dog, the tail of a horse, and on and on.

There was trouble, however, when the animals had to be taken apart to fry the sausage. Tita refused. The only time she was willing to do it was when the sausage was intended for the Christmas Rolls she loved so much. Then she not only allowed her animals to be **dismantled**, she watched them fry with **glee**.

The sausage for the rolls must be fried over very low heat, so that it cooks thoroughly without getting too brown. When done, remove from the heat and add the sardines, which have been deboned. Any black spots on the skin should also have been **scraped off** with a knife. Combine the onions, chopped chillies and the ground oregano with the sardines. Let the mixture stand before filling the rolls.

Tita enjoyed this step enormously; while the filling was resting, it was very pleasant to **savour** its aroma, for smells have the power to evoke the past, bringing back sounds and even smells that have no match in the present. Tita liked to take a deep breath and let the characteristic smoke and scent transport her through **the recesses of** her memory.

It was useless to try to recall the first time she had smelled one of those rolls – she couldn't possibly because it had been before she was born. It might have been the unusual combination of sardines and sausages that had called to her and made her decide to **trade** the peace of ethereal[7] existence in Mama Elena's belly, for life as her daughter, in order to enter the De la Garza family and share their delicious meals and wonderful sausage.

On Mama Elena's ranch, sausage making was a real ritual. The day before, they started peeling garlic, cleaning chillies and

6 *Spanish*: a square or other large open space with a hard surface in a city or town
7 *formal*: qualities with a delicate beauty that makes them seem not to be part of the real world

grinding spices. All the women in the family had to participate: Mama Elena; her daughters, Gertrudis, Rosaura and Tita; Nacha, the cook; and Chencha, the maid. They gathered around the dining-room table in the afternoon, and between the talking and the joking the time flew by until it started to get dark. Then Mama Elena would say, 'That's it for today.'

For a good listener, it is said, a single word will suffice[8], so when they heard that, they all **sprang** into action. First they had to clear the table; then they had to assign tasks: one collected the chickens, another **drew water** for breakfast from the well, a third was in charge of wood for the stove. There would be no ironing, no embroidery, no sewing that day. When it was all finished, they went to their bedrooms to read, say their prayers, and go to sleep. One afternoon, before Mama Elena told them they could leave the table, Tita, who was then fifteen, announced in a trembling voice that Pedro Muzquiz would like to come and speak with her …

After an endless silence during which Tita's soul shrank[9], Mama Elena asked, 'And why should this gentleman want to talk to me?'

Tita's answer could barely be heard. 'I don't know.'

Mama Elena threw her a look that seemed to Tita to contain all the years of repression that had flowed over the family, and said, 'If he intends to ask for your hand, tell him not to bother. He'll be wasting his time and mine too. You know perfectly well that being the youngest daughter means you have to take care of me until the day I die.'

With that Mama Elena got slowly to her feet, put her glasses in her apron, and said in a tone of final command: 'That's it for today.'

Tita knew discussion was not one of the forms of communication permitted in Mama Elena's household, but even so, for the first time in her life, she intended to protest her mother's ruling.

8 *formal* be enough
9 *literary*: move back from someone, especially because you are frightened or nervous (normally *shrink* means get smaller)

'But in my opinion –'

'You don't have an opinion, and that's all I want to hear about it. For generations, not a single person in my family has ever questioned this tradition, and no daughter of mine is going to be the one to start.'

Tita lowered her head, and the realization of her fate struck her as forcibly as her tears struck the table. From then on they knew, she and the table, that they could never **have even the slightest say** in the unknown forces that fated[10] Tita to bow before her mother's absurd decision, and the table to continue to receive the bitter tears that she had first shed on the day of her birth.

Still Tita did not submit. Doubts and anxieties sprang to her mind. For one thing, she wanted to know who had started this family tradition. It would be nice if she could let that genius know about one little **flaw** in this perfect plan for taking care of women in their old age. If Tita couldn't marry and have children, who would take care of her when she got old? Was there a solution in a case like that? Or is a daughter who stays home and takes care of her mother not expected to survive too long after the parent's death? And what about a woman who marries and can't have children, who will take care of her? And besides, she'd like to know what kind of studies had established that the youngest daughter and not the eldest is best suited to care for their mother. Had the opinion of the daughter affected by the plan ever been taken into account? If she couldn't marry, was she at least allowed to experience love? Or not even that?

Tita knew perfectly well that all these questions would have to be buried for ever in the **archive** of questions that have no answers. In the De la Garza family, one obeyed – immediately. Ignoring Tita completely, a very angry Mama Elena left the kitchen, and for the next week she didn't speak a single word to her.

What passed for communication between them resumed[11] when Mama Elena, who was inspecting the clothes each of the

10 *uncommon*: if something fates you, it determines what will happen to you
11 *formal*: started again after being stopped temporarily

women had been sewing, discovered that Tita's creation, which was the most perfect, had not been basted before it was sewed.

'Congratulations,' she said, 'your stitches are perfect – but you didn't baste it, did you?'

'No,' answered Tita, astonished that the sentence[12] of silence had been revoked.

'Then go and rip it out. Baste it and sew it again and then come and show it to me. And remember that the lazy man and the stingy[13] man end up walking their road twice.'

'But that's if a person makes a mistake, and you yourself said a moment ago that my sewing was –'

'Are you starting with your rebelliousness again? It's enough that you have the audacity to break the rules in your sewing.'

'I'm sorry, Mami. I won't ever do it again.'

With that Tita succeeded in calming Mama Elena's anger. For once she had been very careful; she had called her *Mami* in the correct tone of voice. Mama Elena felt that the word *Mama* had a disrespectful sound to it, and so, from the time they were little, she had ordered her daughters to use the word *Mami* when speaking to her. The only one who resisted, the only one who said the word without the proper deference was Tita, which had earned her plenty of slaps. But how perfectly she had said it this time! Mama Elena took comfort in the hope that she had finally managed to subdue her youngest daughter.

Unfortunately her hope was short-lived, for the very next day Pedro Muzquiz appeared at the house, his esteemed[14] father at his side, to ask for Tita's hand in marriage. His arrival caused a huge uproar, as his visit was completely unexpected. Several days earlier Tita had sent Pedro a message via Nacha's brother asking him to abandon his suit[15]. The brother **swore** he had delivered the message to Pedro, and yet there they were, in the house. Mama Elena received them in the living room; she was

12 *legal*: a punishment given by a judge, usually involving a period of time that a person must spend in prison. If it is revoked, it is cancelled.
13 *informal*: unwilling to spend, give or use a lot of money
14 *very formal*: admired and respected
15 *formal, old-fashioned*: if a man abandons his suit, he gives up his intentions to marry someone

extremely polite and explained why it was impossible for Tita to marry.

'But if you really want Pedro to get married, allow me to suggest my daughter Rosaura, who's just two years older than Tita. *She* is one hundred per cent available, and ready for marriage …'

At that Chencha almost dropped right on to Mama Elena the tray containing coffee and cookies, which she had carried into the living room. Excusing herself, she rushed back to the kitchen, where Tita, Rosaura and Gertrudis were waiting for her to fill them in on every detail about what was going on in the living room. She burst headlong[16] into the room, and they all stopped what they were doing, so as not to miss a word she said.

They were together in the kitchen making Christmas Rolls. As the name implies, these rolls are usually prepared around Christmas, but today they were being prepared in honour of Tita's birthday. She would soon be sixteen years old, and she wanted to celebrate with one of her favourite dishes.

'Isn't that something? Your ma talks about being ready for marriage like she was dishing up a plate of enchiladas! And the worst thing is, they're completely different! You can't just switch tacos and enchiladas like that!'

Chencha kept up this kind of running commentary as she told the others – in her own way, of course – about the scene she had just witnessed. Tita knew Chencha sometimes exaggerated and distorted things, so she **held** her aching heart **in check**. She would not accept what she had just heard. **Feigning** calm, she continued cutting the rolls for her sisters and Nacha to fill.

It is best to use home-made rolls. Hard rolls can easily be obtained from a bakery, but they should be small; the larger ones are unsuited for this recipe. After filling the rolls, bake for ten minutes and serve hot. For best results, leave the rolls out overnight, wrapped in a cloth, so that the grease from the sausage soaks into the bread.

While Tita finished wrapping her next day's rolls, Mama Elena came into the kitchen and informed them that she had agreed to Pedro's marriage – to Rosaura.

16 *mainly literary*: very quickly and without looking where you are going

Hearing Chencha's story confirmed, Tita felt her body fill with a wintry **chill**: in one sharp, quick **blast** she was so cold and dry her cheeks burned and turned red, red as the apples beside her. That overpowering chill lasted a long time, and she could find no respite[17], not even when Nacha told her what she had overheard as she escorted Don Pascual Muzquiz and his son to the ranch's gate. Nacha followed them, walking as quietly as she could in order to hear the conversation between father and son. Don Pascual and Pedro were walking slowly, speaking in low, controlled, angry voices.

'Why did you do that, Pedro? It will look ridiculous, your agreeing to marry Rosaura. What happened to the eternal love you swore to Tita? Aren't you going to keep that **vow**?'

'Of course I'll keep it. When you're told there's no way you can marry the woman you love, and your only hope of being near her is to marry her sister, wouldn't you do the same?'

Nacha didn't manage to hear the answer; Pulque, the ranch dog, went running by, barking at a rabbit he mistook for a cat.

'So you intend to marry without love?'

'No, Papa, I am going to marry with a great love for Tita that will never die.'

Their voices grew less and less audible, drowned out by the crackling of dried leaves beneath their feet. How strange that Nacha, who was quite **hard of hearing** by that time, should have claimed to have heard this conversation. Still, Tita thanked Nacha for telling her – but that did not alter the icy feelings she began to have for Pedro. It is said that the deaf can't hear but can understand. Perhaps Nacha only heard what everyone else was afraid to say. Tita could not get to sleep that night; she could not find the words for what she was feeling. How unfortunate that black holes in space had not yet been discovered, for then she might have understood the black hole in the centre of her chest, infinite coldness flowing through it.

Whenever she closed her eyes she saw scenes from last Christmas, the first time Pedro and his family had been invited

17 *formal*: a short period of rest from having to deal with a difficult or unpleasant situation

to dinner; the scenes grew more and more **vivid**, and the cold within her grew sharper. Despite the time that had passed since that evening, she remembered it perfectly: the sounds, the smells, the way her new dress had **grazed** the freshly waxed floor, the look Pedro gave her ... that look! She had been walking to the table carrying a tray of egg-yolk candies when she first felt his hot **gaze** burning her skin. She turned her head, and her eyes met Pedro's. It was then she understood how dough feels when it is plunged into boiling oil. The heat that invaded her body was so real she was afraid she would start to bubble – her face, her stomach, her heart, her breasts – like batter, and unable to endure his gaze she lowered her eyes and hastily crossed the room, to where Gertrudis was pedalling the pianola[18], playing a waltz called 'The Eyes of Youth'[19]. She set her tray on a little table in the middle of the room, picked up a glass of Noyo **liqueur** that was in front of her, hardly aware of what she was doing, and sat down next to Paquita Lobo, the De la Garzas' neighbour. But even that distance between herself and Pedro was not enough; she felt her blood **pulsing**, **searing** her veins. A deep flush suffused[20] her face and no matter how she tried she could not find a place for her eyes to rest. Paquita saw that something was bothering her, and with a look of great concern, she asked, 'That liqueur is pretty strong, isn't it?'

'Pardon me?'

'You look a little **woozy**, Tita. Are you feeling all right?'

'Yes, thank you.'

'You're old enough to have a little drink on a special occasion, but tell me, you little devil, did your mama say it was OK? I can see you're excited – you're shaking – and I'm sorry but I must say you'd better not have any more. You wouldn't want to make a fool of yourself.'

That was the last straw! To have Paquita Lobo think she was drunk. She couldn't allow the tiniest suspicion to remain in Paquita's mind or she might tell her mother. Tita's fear of her

18 a piano that plays music by itself, worked by pressing foot pedals up and down
19 a popular waltz by Mexican composer, Arturo Tolentino
20 *literary*: spread over or through something

mother was enough to make her forget Pedro for a moment, and she applied herself to convincing Paquita, any way she could, that she was thinking clearly, that her mind was alert. She chatted with her, she **gossiped**, she made small talk. She even told her the recipe for this Noyo liqueur which was supposed to have had such an effect on her. The spirit is made by soaking four ounces of peaches and half a pound of apricots in water for twenty-four hours to loosen the skin; next, they are peeled, crushed and steeped in hot water for fifteen days. Then the spirit is distilled. After two and a half pounds of sugar have been completely dissolved in the water, four ounces of orange-flower water are added, and the mixture is stirred and strained. And so there would be no lingering doubts about her mental and physical well-being, she reminded Paquita, as if it were just an **aside**, that the water containers held 2.016 litres, no more and no less.

So when Mama Elena came over to ask Paquita if she was being properly entertained, she replied enthusiastically.

'Oh yes, perfectly! You have such wonderful daughters. Such fascinating conversation!'

Mama Elena sent Tita to the kitchen to get something for the guests. Pedro '**happened**' to be walking by at that moment and he offered his help. Tita rushed off to the kitchen without a word. His presence made her extremely uncomfortable. He followed her in, and she quickly sent him off with one of the trays of delicious snacks that had been waiting on the kitchen table.

She would never forget the moment their hands accidentally touched as they both slowly bent down to pick up the same tray.

That was when Pedro confessed his love.

'Senorita Tita, I would like to take advantage of this opportunity to be alone with you to tell you that I am deeply in love with you. I know this declaration is **presumptuous**, and that it's quite sudden, but it's so hard to get near you that I decided to tell you tonight. All I ask is that you tell me whether I can hope to win your love.'

'I don't know what to say … give me time to think.'

'No, no, I can't! I need an answer now: you don't have to think about love; you either feel it or you don't. I am a man of few words, but my word is my pledge[21]. I swear that my love for you will last for ever. What about you? Do you feel the same way about me?'

'Yes!'

Yes, a thousand times. From that night on she would love him for ever. And now she had to give him up. It wasn't decent to desire your sister's future husband. She had to try to put him out of her mind somehow, so she could get to sleep. She started to eat the Christmas roll Nacha had left on her bureau[22], along with a glass of milk; this **remedy** had proven effective many times. Nacha, with all her experience, knew that for Tita there was no pain that wouldn't disappear if she ate a delicious Christmas roll. But this time it didn't work. She felt no relief from the **hollow** sensation in her stomach. Just the opposite, a wave of **nausea** flowed over her. She realized that the hollow sensation was not hunger but an icy feeling of **grief**. She had to get rid of that terrible sensation of cold. First she put on a wool robe and a heavy cloak. The cold still gripped her. Then she put on felt slippers and another two shawls. No good. Finally she went to her sewing box and pulled out the bedspread she had started the day Pedro first spoke of marriage. A bedspread like that, a crocheted one, takes about a year to complete. Exactly the length of time Pedro and Tita had planned to wait before getting married. She decided to use the yarn, not to let it go to waste, and so she worked on the bedspread and wept furiously, weeping and working until dawn and threw it over herself. It didn't help at all. Not that night, nor many others, for as long as she lived, could she free herself from that cold.

21 *old-fashioned*: a promise
22 a piece of furniture used for storing clothes. In British English it is for writing or storing paperwork.

Post-reading activities

Understanding the story

1   Use these questions to help you check that you have understood the story.

Tita's childhood

1   How does the story begin? Why does it not continue this way?
2   What is the storyteller's relationship to the main character, Tita?
3   List the members of the De la Garza household and the relationships between them.
4   What is unusual about Tita's birth?
5   How does Nacha make good use of Tita's birth?
6   Why is it decided that Nacha should look after feeding the baby?
7   Why is the kitchen so important to Tita?
8   What happens when the sisters play in the kitchen? Who gets the blame?

Pedro

9   Tita says that she doesn't know why Pedro Musquiz is coming to speak with her mother. Is this true? Why does she say it?
10 How does Mama Elena behave towards Tita after the news about Pedro? How does Tita calm her down?
11 Why is Pedro's arrival unexpected?
12 How do the sisters hear what Mama Elena and Pedro are talking about before their mother informs them?
13 Why are they making Christmas rolls that day?
14 What arrangement is made between Mama Elena and Pedro? How does Tita react to the news?
15 Why does Pedro agree to Mama Elena's idea, according to Chencha?
16 When did Tita and Pedro first declare their love for one another?
17 How does Tita react to Pedro looking at her at the party? What does Paquita think?
18 Why does Tita tell Paquita that water containers hold 2.016 litres?
19 What reason is given for why Tita disagrees with Pedro's decision?
20 How does Nacha try to help? Does it work?
21 What is unusual about the cold that Tita feels?

2 **Use these questions to help you check that you have understood the recipe.**

22 What is unusual about the recipe?
23 What can you do to stop yourself from crying as you chop onions, according to the storyteller?
24 Why should you cook the sausages slowly?
25 What are some ingredients in the sausage?
26 What preparation is there for the fish?
27 What cooking tips are given concerning the rolls?
28 Put these steps in the making of Christmas rolls in order:
   a) Add the sardines.
   b) Bake in the oven for 10 minutes.
   c) Eat with a glass of milk!
   d) Fill the rolls.
   e) Fry the sausage over a low heat.
   f) Leave overnight.
   g) Leave the mixture to stand for a while.
   h) Mix in the onions, chillies and oregano.
29 Would you like this recipe? Why/Why not?

Language study

Grammar

Colons and semi-colons

A colon is a punctuation mark which looks like this :

A semi-colon looks like this ;

Colons are used to separate two clauses where the second clause explains, expands on or gives examples of something mentioned in the first clause:

> *Her sisters were just the opposite: to them, Tita's world seemed full of unknown dangers, and they were terrified of it.*

To replace the colon, you could use a phrase with a reference device, such as *which* or *this*:

> *Her sisters were just the opposite, **which is to say that** to them, Tita's world seemed full of unknown dangers, and they were terrified of it.*

Look at another example. Here, the first clause states that there is a problem. The second clause says what the problem is:

Tita was in love with Pedro but she had just one problem: he was going to marry her sister.

It could be rewritten:

Tita was in love with Pedro but she had just one problem, **which was that** *he was going to marry her sister.*

Colons are used to introduce lists when the list provides extra information about something mentioned before the colon:

Despite the time that had passed since that evening, she remembered it perfectly: the sounds, the smells, the way her new dress had grazed the freshly waxed floor, the look Pedro gave her ... that look!

Colons are often used to introduce direct speech:

With that Mama Elena got slowly to her feet, put her glasses in her apron, and said in a tone of final command: 'That's it for today.'

Colons are used in academic writing when quoting extracts from a book which illustrate or exemplify a point you are making. Notice, for example, how colons have been used in this section to introduce the extracts from the story.

Colons are also used to separate the title and subtitle of books:

Like Water for Chocolate: A Novel in Monthly Installments with Recipes, Romances and Home Remedies

Semi-colons connect two clauses in which the second clause relates to the first but does not refer specifically to something mentioned in the first:

Tita enjoyed this step enormously; while the filling was resting, it was very pleasant to savour its aroma

Notice how the two clauses are independent of each other. A full stop can replace the semi-colon:

Tita enjoyed this step enormously. While the filling was resting, it was very pleasant to savour its aroma

However, notice that the semi-colon draws attention to how the two clauses are related; the full stop does not.

You could also use a comma with a conjunction (like *and*) to replace it:

Tita enjoyed this step enormously, **and** *while the filling was resting, it was very pleasant to savour its aroma*

The difference between the semi-colon and using a comma with *and* is one of style. In the examples above, do you prefer the semi-colon or the comma and conjunction?

Semi-colons are also used to separate items in lists when the items are long:

> *Her eating habits, for example, were attuned to the kitchen routine: in the morning, when she could smell that the beans were ready; at midday, when she sensed the water was ready for plucking the chickens; and in the afternoon, when the dinner bread was baking, Tita knew it was time for her to be fed.*

1 Punctuate the following extracts using colons and semi-colons where appropriate. You may need more than one punctuation mark.

1 *Tita was so sensitive to onions, any time they were being chopped, they say she would just cry and cry when she was still in my great-grandmother's belly her sobs were so loud that even Nacha could hear them easily.*

2 *All the women in the family had to participate Mama Elena her daughters, Gertrudis, Rosaura and Tita Nacha, the cook and Chencha, the maid.*

3 *First they had to clear the table, then they had to assign tasks one collected the chickens, another drew water for breakfast from the well, a third was in charge of wood for the stove.*

4 *Tita could not get to sleep that night she could not find the words for what she was feeling.*

2 Do the same for the following sentences.

1 The reason you should leave them overnight is simple they taste better!

2 You'll love everything about this meal the smell of coriander in the salad the way the serrano chilli contrasts with the cooling, creamy yoghurt dressing the red, green and white colours on the plate.

3 I knew the book was about Mexican food but I didn't realize that its full name is *Hot and Spicy A culinary tour of Mexico*.

4 In the end, they couldn't make the recipe Carmen had forgotten to buy chorizo.

5 Mexican food can be surprisingly healthy many dishes contain beans, or avocado, and they eat very little red meat.

6 Nutritionist Victor Lindlahr famously declared 'You are what you eat'.

Vocabulary

Common expressions

3 Look at the common expressions (1–12) and match them with the definitions (a–l).

1 **come/spring to mind**
Tita questions the decision that she cannot marry:
Doubts and anxieties sprang to her mind.

2 **for one thing**
Tita starts to lists the arguments against the decision:
For one thing, she wanted to know who had started this family tradition.

3 **give/throw someone a (dirty) look**
Mama Elena is angry that Tita wants to marry Pedro:
Mama Elena threw her a look that seemed to Tita to contain years of repression

4 **go to waste**
Tita continues making the bedspread:
She decided to use the yarn, not to let it go to waste.

5 **know something perfectly well**
Mama Elena is annoyed with Tita:
'You know perfectly well that being the youngest daughter means you have to take care of me until the day I die.'

6 **not the slightest**
Tita thinks about the lack of power in her own life:
She knew she could never have even the slightest say in the unknown forces that fated her.

7 **on top of**
Elena is too busy to spend time with Tita:
… without having to worry about feeding a newborn baby on top of everything else.

8 **the next thing you know**
The problem with onions:
Once the tears begin to well up, the next thing you know you just can't stop.

9 **small talk**
At the party with Paquita:
She chatted with her, she gossiped, she made small talk.

10 **the last straw**
Tita is having difficulty controlling herself at the party:
That was the last straw! To have Paquita Lobo think she was drunk.

11 **throw yourself into something**
The girls are playing in the kitchen:
Gertrudis threw herself into it with the enthusiasm she always showed where rhythm, movement or music were involved.

12 **to take something into account**
Tita is building her argument against staying with her mother:
Had the opinion of the daughter affected by the plan ever been taken into account?

a) be spoiled or thrown away
b) remember something suddenly or start to think about it
c) start giving all your energy or attention to doing an activity
d) in addition to something else
e) informal conversation about things that are not important
f) consider something when you are trying to make a decision
g) look at someone in a particular way, especially in a way that shows that you are angry with them
h) none at all
i) the final event in a series of events that causes an angry or violent reaction
j) used for saying that a situation happens very quickly when you do not expect it
k) used for saying in an annoyed way that someone should already know something
l) used when mentioning one reason for something as an example, when there are several reasons

4 **Use the expressions (1–12) in 3 to complete these sentences.**
1 .... all his financial problems, his wife left him.
2 I opened the door and .... there were police officers in my house.
3 After my girlfriend left me, I .... my work.
4 She asked me for ideas, but nothing ....
5 He's .... I don't know why; I haven't done anything wrong.
6 You .... that's not allowed. I've told you a thousand times!
7 I was so tired I had .... difficulty getting to sleep.
8 Many people don't take the time to read contracts. ...., they're often in very tiny print. And for another, they're incredibly boring!
9 It's a complex problem. We'll need to .... many factors.

10 When he didn't come home again that night, it was ....

11 I don't remember what we talked about. Nothing important. You
    know, just ....

12 The cherries will just .... if we don't pick them soon.

Literary analysis

Plot

1 The novel recounts the life of the main character, Tita. What key
   biographical events are described in Chapter One?

2 Are the events described in chronological order? What is the effect
   of this?

3 What do you think happens in the rest of the novel?

4 What does the extract tell us about love and marriage in early
   twentieth-century Mexico?

5 Now that you have read the first chapter, do you feel motivated to
   read the rest of the novel? Why/Why not?

The role of food in the story

6 Where do the important moments in the extract take place? How
   is food involved in these events?

7 What are the main ingredients and flavours in the dishes described
   in the extract? In what way are these suitable for the type of story
   that is told?

8 Look at the following extracts. Why are apples and dough
   mentioned at these points? What effect does this have?

   *Hearing Chencha's story confirmed, Tita … was so cold and dry her
   cheeks burned and turned red, red as the apples beside her.*

   *She turned her head, and her eyes met Pedro's. It was then she
   understood how dough feels when it is plunged into boiling oil.*

9 In what ways does food unite the characters? In what ways does it
   cause divisions?

10 Food is often equated to emotions in the extract. Find some
    instances of this – what do they tell us about how the characters
    are feeling?

Character

11 The first piece of information we are given about Tita is that she 'was so sensitive to onions, any time they were being chopped, she would just cry and cry'. Think of other situations in the story where she has a strong physical response to important events. What are her responses? What does this tell us about her?

12 Who does Tita spend most of her childhood with? What does this suggest about her relationship with her mother and her position in the De la Garza household?

13 Write three adjectives to describe Tita's mother, Elena. Can you think of any reasons why she might be like this?

14 What do we know about her sisters, Gertrudis and Rosaura?

15 What do we know about the maid, Chencha?

16 How many male characters are there in the extract?

17 Pedro is the only man that we learn much about. Is he a realistic character in your opinion? Does he conform to any stereotypes that you know?

18 Can you understand his reason for marrying Rosaura? Do you think he made a wise decision? Why/Why not?

Narration

19 The extract begins as a recipe. How much of the recipe do we get at the start? Find other instances when either the story interrupts a recipe or a recipe interrupts the story. What effect do these interruptions have?

20 The storyteller addresses the reader directly at the beginning of the story, using *you*. What effect does this have?

21 What impression do you get of the storyteller? Do you think the storyteller is a man or woman? Why?

Style

22 The style of the story switches frequently from narrating the action to giving recipes. Decide whether the following stylistic elements are more typical of a) the narrative or b) recipes.
   1 a range of past tenses
   2 use of the passive voice
   3 short, simple sentences
   4 a variety of long, multi-clause sentences and short, simple sentences
   5 descriptive adjectives
   6 use of the imperative
   7 linkers such as 'next' and 'after this' to help the reader understand the sequence of actions
   8 an impersonal tone
   9 a wide range of linkers of different types

23 Read the paragraph beginning 'The sausage for the rolls …' on page 133. Find examples of the elements for recipes listed above.

24 In the following extract, what is unusual about the comparison being made? What message does it convey to you?

   Tita lowered her head, and the realization of her fate struck her as forcibly as her tears struck the table. From then on they knew, she and the table, that they could never have even the slightest say in the unknown forces that fated Tita to bow before her mother's absurd decision, and the table to continue to receive the bitter tears that she had first shed on the day of her birth.

25 Read the paragraph that begins: 'Still Tita did not submit …' on page 135. Tita calls the person who had started the tradition that the youngest daughter cannot marry a 'genius', which she clearly does not believe. Find other instances of saying the opposite to what she means in that paragraph. What effect does it create? How do the questions she asks contribute to this effect?

Magic realism

Magic realism is a common type of literature or cinema in Latin American fiction in which very strange things happen in ordinary situations, as they do in dreams. The story is realistic except for occasional fantastical events. An example of this is during Tita's birth. The storyteller presents a story about her great-aunt as if it were historical biography.

26 What happens at her birth that is fantastical?
27 What other events and experiences described in the extract are
    not very realistic? Do these strange events improve or spoil your
    reading experience?
28 Read the following extract:

> **The way Nacha tells it**, *Tita was literally washed into this world on
> a great tide of tears* …

  What is the storyteller's attitude to the more fantastical events in
  the story? What are your reactions as a reader?
29 Does the style of the extract appeal to you? Why/Why not?

*Guidance to the above literary terms, answer keys to all the exercises and
activities, plus a wealth of other reading-practice material, can be found at:
www.macmillanenglish.com/readers.*

A *Piece of Pie*

by Damon Runyon

About the author

Damon Runyon's name is closely connected to the city of New York. An adjective, *Runyonesque*, exists to describe a romantic world in and around the city's famous street of theatres, Broadway, with its actors, gangsters, gamblers[1] and dancers. When he died in 1946, the ashes that remained after his body had been burnt were illegally scattered from an aeroplane over the streets of Manhattan. However, Runyon was not born in New York, nor was his life as glamorous or as easy-going as those of his characters.

Alfred Damon Runyan came from a family of newspaper men in a small town, coincidentally called Manhattan, in Kansas in the middle of the United States. His grandfather worked in the print room of the local newspaper, and his father later ran a paper there. In 1882, when young Alfred was only two, they moved west to Colorado where he spent the rest of his childhood. It was a difficult family: his father drank; his mother died when he was only eight, and his sisters went away to live with their grandmother. He started working for his father in the print rooms of the newspaper when he was still a boy and remained a journalist for the rest of his life.

Before he came to New York, Runyan worked in Denver, Colorado. In one of his articles his name was misspelled Runyon, but he didn't correct it and chose to stay Runyon for the rest of his career. Later, working in New York, his full name was too long to fit on the line so Alfred was dropped. He became 'Damon Runyon'. In his stories, the characters' names are rarely their real names, and they sometimes change their name. Invention and reinvention was for Runyon not just a writing technique, but a part of real life, too.

One example of this inventiveness was as a sports journalist. Runyon wrote articles about the baseball matches of the New York Giants for several newspapers, but he turned his job of reporting the games into an art form, finding funny stories in and around the baseball pitch,

1 someone who likes risking their money on the result of races and competitions

giving players and managers interesting nicknames and describing spectators in the crowd. His articles added colour to the sport that didn't exist before.

In private, too, he invented stories to make life more interesting. He married twice: with his first wife, Ellen Egan, he had two children; but he left her in 1928 for a young Mexican actress, Patrice Amadi, who he had met years before in Mexico when she was just twelve years old. He had given her money for her education and told her to come to New York when she was older. When she unexpectedly arrived in town, Runyon decided that she could not be a poor girl from Mexico. He recreated her past and they pretended that she was a Spanish countess, a member of the European upper class. They even pretended that she owned one of the biggest diamonds in the world which they insured for $200,000. Years later, she was robbed and was awarded the insurance money, despite the fact that the diamond had never existed!

Runyon's New York was populated with people who did not have normal jobs, or children; they were 'people on the wrong side of the law' according to his biographer, Jimmy Breslin. 'He wrote stories as if there were no such thing as a Monday morning and people had to get up for work'. It was an invented world that caught the imagination of readers, radio producers and filmmakers. Twenty-six of his short stories were turned into films, the most famous being *Guys and Dolls* (actually a combination of two of his stories), and his influence continues today in gangster films and the popular imagination.

He died aged sixty-six of throat cancer due to his heavy smoking. His friend and radio presenter, Walter Winchell, used his show to raise public awareness of cancer and asked listeners for money to help research the disease. *The Damon Runyon Cancer Research Foundation* was one of the first organisations to promote research into cancer and has invested $270 million into scientific investigation since Runyon's death.

Runyon left us more than just lively stories and memorable characters. He created new forms of expression in his dialogues and descriptions, and many informal words and phrases that started life in his stories have become part of everyday speech. A good dictionary should be able to help you understand some of them: *to give someone the heave-ho*; *to have something in spades*; *no dice*; *a zillion*; *the dream team*. In fact, a total of 231 words and expressions in the *Oxford English Dictionary* are attributed to him.

About the story

A *Piece of Pie* was first published in *Colliers Magazine,* a popular American weekly magazine, in 1937. The following year it appeared in a collection of his short stories, *Take It Easy.* Since then it has been adapted for radio several times; you can find audio versions of the story online to listen to the New York accent and Runyon's special style, 'Runyonese', as it is spoken.

A note about 'Runyonese'

Damon Runyon is famous not only for the plots of his stories but also for his writing style, which is very unusual. He almost never uses past forms, the perfect or continuous aspects, or conditional structures with *would*, preferring the present tense and *will* instead. Contracted forms such as 'he's' or 'I'm' are never used, either. His writing sometimes contains invented phrases and slang (words and expressions that are very informal and not considered suitable for more formal situations). A lot of Runyon's slang comes from the world of horse racing and particular groups living in New York, so it is only understandable in its context. His characters use this slang in their speech but often mix it with formal words to sound more important and clever, often with a comic effect. There are activities to help you understand the slang and formal vocabulary in the Pre-reading section below. In the Post-reading section there are activities that explore the use of tense in this special style called 'Runyonese'.

Background information

Food in the story: eating contests

Eating contests are a popular form of competition in the United States, Canada and Japan. In the United States, they were traditionally held at county fairs. These are shows where the public can come and see farm animals and watch sports associated with agriculture. Nowadays, competitive eating is more commercialized: there are events on television, an international federation that controls the 'sport' and even world champions.

Although competitive eating is seen as light-hearted fun by most people, there are others who criticize it because it encourages overeating and the health risks related to obesity. When eating much more than you need is seen as a bad habit, it is known as gluttony. Also, some people are unhappy that while the contestants eat too much, there are many people in the world who do not have enough to eat and suffer from undernourishment.

There is a recipe for pumpkin pie on page 192.

Gambling

In many countries it is common for people to risk money by betting – saying what they think will happen, especially in a race or game. They lose the money if they are wrong and win more if they are right. For example, it is possible to bet, or wager, money on who you think will win a sports event like a football match or horse race. Gambling, as the activity of betting is known, is big business, and people who accept bets are called bookmakers. If you win the bet, you go to the bookmakers to settle the bet and they will pay you your winnings.

How much money you win will depend on how likely the bookmaker thinks it is that your team, player or horse will win its match or race. If you bet on someone that has an outside chance (a small chance) of winning, the amount you win will be larger. If you choose the favourite to win (the team, player or horse most likely to win), you will not win as much money. The chance of winning is expressed in numbers, such as 'two to one' or 'six to five'. If you have made a risky bet, you may want to limit the amount of money you could lose by betting on the other team as well. This is called 'hedging' your bets.

Gambling can become an addiction and many people disapprove of the practice. It is a crime to gamble in some countries, and in the United States, there are two states, Utah and Hawaii, where gambling is illegal.

Horse racing

Horse racing is one of the sports most closely related to gambling. One scene in the story is set at a racecourse, the place where horse races are held. These can be on a flat course or they can be jump races, which involve the horses jumping over hedges. Horse racing is also important in the story because the main characters are gamblers and use racing expressions to describe the eaters in the eating contest. So, for example, a horse's ability to run fast is known as its 'form', and so is the eaters' ability to eat well. It is important for professional horse players, or gamblers, to 'get a line on the horses' form'; in other words, they must study the horses before they can decide which ones to bet on. This is equally true before the eating contest. How the eaters actually perform in the contest is described as their 'showing', the same word that is used for horses' performance in races.

Summary

It may help you to know something about what happens in the story before you read it. Don't worry, this summary does not tell you how the story ends!

The story is set in New York and Boston in 1937. The storyteller and a friend of his, known as Horse Thief, are at a restaurant in Boston when they hear some men at a nearby table talking about someone who can eat a lot of food, a man called Joel Duffle. Horse Thief decides to speak to them; he also knows someone who can eat like that, so he challenges them to a bet that his man can eat more food than theirs. He gives them $1000 as a forfeit (money he will have to pay if the contest does not happen) and bets them $10,000. The men from Boston accept the bet and they decide on a time and place for the contest, four weeks later.

The man that Horse Thief has planned to compete in the contest is called Nicely-Nicely Jones. They look for him in the local bars and restaurants but no one has seen him. Eventually, the two men find him living with a woman called Miss Hilda Slocum. They do not recognize him because he is so thin. When they tell him about the contest, he is very sad because he is unable to help them; Miss Slocum has put him on a very strict diet. She says she will only marry him if he loses lots of weight. There is no possibility that Nicely-Nicely can compete. It looks as if Horse Thief will lose his money.

However, luck is on Horse Thief's side; he is at Belmont Park racecourse on Long Island in New York, when he gives a man some advice about which horse to bet on. When the horse wins the race, the man is very grateful to him, and they start talking. He is Miss Slocum's boss, so Horse Thief explains the eating contest and the problem with Miss Slocum. The man is very interested in the contest and promises to help. The next day, Miss Slocum calls Horse Thief with a suggestion. Although she still refuses to allow her future husband to compete, she has a friend who can replace him … but will she live up to expectations?

Pre-reading activities

Key vocabulary

Eating contests, gambling and horse-racing terms are dealt with in the section on Background information (page 154). This section will help you familiarize yourself with some of the more specific vocabulary used in the story. You may want to use it to help you before you start reading, or as a revision exercise after you have finished the story.

Food

1 **Here are some of the food items mentioned in the story. Read the words and their definitions. Which items might ...**
a) be the principal ingredient in a main meal?
b) accompany meat as part of a main meal?
c) be eaten as a dessert after a main meal?

asparagus a long thin green vegetable whose stems and pointed ends are eaten

biscuit *US English*: a small round soft bread roll

celery a pale green vegetable with a group of long stems that are eaten raw or cooked

clam a small shellfish

corn on the cob the seed head of a maize plant, cooked and eaten as a vegetable

dumplings small balls of flour and fat cooked in boiling water, often eaten with meat or added to soup

knuckle a piece of meat from an animal's lower leg

lima bean a flat pale green bean that is grown in America

lobster a large, expensive shellfish with a long body and two large parts like arms called claws

muffin a small sweet cake that sometimes contains fruit

pumpernickel a type of dark rye bread

sauerkraut a German food made from cabbage

shortcake a biscuit made with flour, butter and sugar that is often served with fruit and cream

2 **From the list above, what is your overall impression of the food that is eaten in the story?**

Ways to describe food

3 Read the definitions below. Write next to each at least one type of food that might be cooked this way or contain this type of ingredient.

broiled *US English*: grilled or barbecued

fricassee a meal that consists of pieces of fried meat served in a thick white sauce

mashed boiled in water, crushed and then mixed with milk and butter until smooth

stewed cooked slowly in liquid

whipped with air mixed into it, so that it is very light

wholewheat made of flour that contains all the wheat grain including the outer part

Imperial measurements

In the United States, imperial units are used to measure food and other things, not metric units such as kilograms or litres.

4 What types of food or other things might be measured with the following units?

1 gallon = 3.8 litres
1 quart = 946 millilitres (there are 4 quarts in a gallon)
1 pound = 454 grams
1 ounce = 28 grams (there are 16 ounces in a pound)
1 foot = 30 centimetres
1 inch = 2.5 centimetres (there are 12 inches in a foot)
a dozen = twelve

Competitions

5 Read the paragraph about competitions and find words or phrases in the text that match the definitions (a–j). The definitions are in the order that the words appear in the text.

What do you need to consider when organising a competition? Firstly, the terms of any competition must be decided in good time to ensure that all contenders are familiar with the rules and happy that the match will be fair. It would be a shame if one side lost on a technicality. For this reason, too, it is important to have a neutral judge, especially when one team claims a foul. No one likes to see an easy game, so the best contests have opponents who are well matched. Few games finish with both sides dead even; either the result is clear at the end of the time limit, or one side throws in the towel. But if it does result in a tie, there should be an agreed way of deciding a winner.

a) the conditions of an agreement that the people making it accept
b) someone who competes with other people for a prize
c) a minor detail of the rules that can lead to an unfair result
d) not supporting one side or the other
e) say that the other team has done something that is not allowed by the rules
f) someone who is competing against you
g) be chosen to compete against an opponent of a similar level
h) completely the same, with neither side winning
i) stop taking part in a competition because you think you cannot win
j) a result of a competition in which each person has the same number of points

Slang words and expressions

Many of the words and expressions that the writer uses are slang. That is, they are very informal and are not considered suitable in more formal situations. They were used by people in New York in the early twentieth century but may be considered old-fashioned nowadays.

6 Read the expressions and definitions in the box. Do you have slang expressions in your own language for any of these things?

> **cad** a man who behaves in an unkind or unfair way, especially towards women
> **clock** notice
> **cop** a police officer
> **dibs, dough** money
> **fodder** food
> **a goner** someone who is certain to die very soon
> **joint** a restaurant, bar, or club, especially one that is cheap and not very nice
> **Judy** a woman
> **licked** easily defeated in a competition
> **out with something** get it out (of your pocket, for example)
> **plumb tuckered out** completely tired
> **slap a lip over** eat
> **tap out** use all the money that someone or something has available
> **a tenner** $10 or $10,000

Phrasal verbs

7 **Match the verbs in bold in the sentences (1–10) below with their definitions (a–j)**

1 I **talked** her **into** going to London with me.
2 I was a bit late but I couldn't **let** them **down** completely.
3 It **turns out** that I was right all along.
4 Our teacher is **stepping up** homework now the exams are getting near.
5 She can really **pack** it **away**!
6 Sheila carried a knife to **ward off** attacks.
7 The company is **pulling out** of the personal computer business.
8 We didn't think Austin would **show up**.
9 The family **put up** £15,000 towards the cost of her medical treatment.
10 The responsibility of her new job had begun to **weigh on** her.

a) do something to prevent someone or something from harming you
b) persuade someone to do something
c) make someone disappointed by not doing something that they are expecting you to do
d) be discovered to be something
e) stop being involved in an activity, event, or situation
f) increase something
g) *informal*: to eat a large quantity of food
h) *informal*: to arrive in a place where people are expecting you
i) provide a large amount of money for something
j) make someone worried

Formal words

8 **Match the formal words in bold from the extracts (a–i) with their less formal synonyms (1–9).**

1 eat	4 help	7 lives
2 eating	5 kind, type	8 start
3 eats	6 let in	9 stop

a) *Who is in there **partaking of** this lobster but Horse Thief and me*
b) *Boston is really quite infested with characters of this **nature***
c) *A great eater who **resides** in your fair city*
d) *I **commence** wondering where I can raise a few dibs*
e) *I am unable to **oblige** them*

f) *A customer who is about to **consume** some strawberry shortcake*

g) *The restaurant is closed and only parties immediately concerned are **admitted***

h) *She **disposes of** her share of the turkey*

i) *I **cease** dieting. I learn my lesson*

Main themes

Before you read the story, you may want to think about some of its main themes. The questions will help you think about the story as you are reading it for the first time. There is more discussion of the main themes in the *Literary analysis* section after the story.

Attitudes to dieting

The story explores differing attitudes to food, how people eat and how much. Most, but not all, of the characters enjoy eating good food and watching others eat.

9 As you read the story, ask yourself the following questions:

a) Who are seen as 'good eaters'? What qualities do they show?

b) What other attitudes to food are described?

Bodies and appearance

We do not find out what all of the main characters look like or what they wear, but when people are described physically in the story, the focus is often on the shape and size of their bodies.

10 Think about these questions while you read:

a) Which characters are described physically?

b) What types of body are represented in the story?

c) Does the storyteller give his opinion about their size?

A *Piece of Pie*

by Damon Runyon

In any eating contest the principals[2] may speak to each other if they wish, though smart eaters never wish to do this, as talking only wastes energy. This is the story of a contestant who spoke to Nicely-Nicely Jones and the surprising results.

On Boylston Street, in the city of Boston, Massachusetts, there is a joint where you can get as nice a broiled lobster as anybody ever slaps a lip over, and who is in there one evening partaking of this **tidbit** but a character by the name of Horse Thief and me.

This Horse Thief is called Horsey for short, and he is not called by this name because he ever steals a horse but because it is the **consensus** of public opinion from coast to coast that he may steal one if the opportunity presents.

Personally I consider Horsey a very fine character, because any time he is holding anything[3] he is willing to share his good fortune with one and all, and at this time in Boston he is holding plenty. It is the time we make the race meeting at Suffolk Downs[4], and Horsey gets to going very good, indeed, and in fact he is now a character of means, and is my host against the broiled lobster.

Well, at a table next to us are four or five characters who all seem to be well-dressed, and **stout**-set, and red-faced, and **prosperous**-looking, and who all speak with the true Boston accent, which consists of many ah's and very few r's. Characters such as these are familiar to anybody who is ever in Boston very much, and they are bound to be politicians, retired cops, or contractors, because Boston is really quite infested with characters of this nature.

2 *uncommon*: the main characters, in this case the contestants
3 when he has a lot of money
4 a racetrack in Boston

I am paying no attention to them, because they are drinking local **ale**, and talking loud, and long ago I learn that when a Boston character is engaged in aleing himself up, it is a good idea to let him alone, because the best you can get out of him is maybe a boff on the beezer[5]. But Horsey is in there on the old Ear-ie[6], and very much interested in their conversation, and finally I listen myself just to hear what is attracting his attention, when one of the characters speaks as follows:

"Well," he says, "I am willing to bet ten thousand dollars that he can outeat anybody in the United States any time."

Now at this, Horsey gets right up and steps over to the table and bows and smiles in a friendly way on one and all, and says:

"Gentlemen," he says, "pardon the intrusion, and excuse me for billing in[7], but," he says, "do I understand you are speaking of a great eater who resides in your fair city?"

Well, these Boston characters all gaze at Horsey in such a **hostile** manner that I am expecting any one of them to get up and request him to let them miss him, but he keeps on bowing and smiling, and they can see that he is a gentleman, and finally one of them says:

"Yes," he says, "we are speaking of a character by the name of Joel Duffle. He is without doubt the greatest eater alive. He just wins a unique wager. He just bets a character from Bangor, Maine, that he can eat a whole window display of oysters in this very restaurant, and he not only eats all the oysters but he then wishes to wager that he can also eat the shells, but," he says, "it seems that the character from Bangor, Maine, unfortunately taps out[8] on the first proposition and has nothing with which to bet on the second."

"Very interesting." Horsey says. "Very interesting, if true, but," he says, "unless my ears deceive me, I hear one of you state that he is willing to wager ten thousand dollars on this eater of yours against anybody in the United States."

---

5   *slang*: a punch on the nose
6   *Runyonese*: listening to their conversation
7   *informal*: (normally *butt in*) join a conversation or activity without being asked to
8   *informal*: have no more money left

"Your ears are perfect," another of the Boston characters says. "I state it, although," he says, "I admit it is a sort of **figure of speech**. But I state it all right," he says, "and never let it be said that a Conway ever pigs it on a betting proposition.⁹"

"Well," Horsey says, "I do not have a tenner on me at the moment, but," he says, "I have here a thousand dollars to put up as a forfeit that I can produce a character who will outeat your party for ten thousand, and as much more as you care to put up."

And with this, Horsey outs with a **bundle** of coarse notes and tosses it on the table, and right away one of the Boston characters, whose name turns out to be Carroll, slaps his hand on the money and says:

"Bet."

Well, now this is prompt action to be sure, and if there is one thing I admire more than anything else, it is action, and I can see that these are characters of true sporting instincts and I commence wondering where I can raise a few dibs to take a piece of Horsey's proposition[10], because of course I know that he has nobody in mind to do the eating for his side but Nicely-Nicely Jones.

And knowing Nicely-Nicely Jones, I am prepared to wager all the money I can possibly raise that he can outeat anything that walks on two legs. In fact, I will take a chance on Nicely-Nicely against anything on four legs, except maybe an elephant, and at that he may give the elephant a photo finish.

I do not say that Nicely-Nicely is the greatest eater in all history, but what I do say is he belongs up there as a contender. In fact, Professor D., who is a professor in a college out West before he turns to playing the horses for a **livelihood**, and who makes a study of history in his time, says he will not be surprised but what Nicely-Nicely figures one-two[11].

Professor D. says we must always remember that Nicely-Nicely eats under the **handicaps** of modern civilization, which require that an eater use a knife and fork, or anyway a knife, while in

9 *Runyonese*: refuse to accept a challenge
10 take a share of Horsey's bet
11 Professor D. thinks that Nicely-Nicely will always be the favourite to win.

the old days eating with the hands was a popular custom and much faster. Professor D. says he has no doubt that under the old rules Nicely-Nicely will hang up a record that will endure through the ages, but of course maybe Professor D. overlays[12] Nicely-Nicely **somewhat**.

Well, now that the match is agreed upon[13], naturally Horsey and the Boston characters begin discussing where it is to take place, and one of the Boston characters suggests a neutral ground, such as New London, Conneticut, or Providence, Rhode Island, but Horsey holds out for New York, and it seems that Boston characters are always ready to visit New York, so he does not meet with any great opposition on this point.

They all agree on a date four weeks later so as to give the principals plenty of time to get ready, although Horsey and I know that this is really unnecessary as far as Nicely-Nicely is concerned, because one thing about him is he is always in condition to eat.

Nicely-Nicely is called by this name because any time anybody asks him how he feels, or how he is doing, he always says nicely, nicely, and the consequence is he goes through life a constant perjurer[14], at least on how he is doing. He is a character who is maybe five feet eight inches tall, and about five feet nine inches wide, and when he is in good shape he will weigh upward of 283 pounds[15]. He is a horse player by trade, and eating is really just a hobby, but he is undoubtedly a wonderful eater even when he is not hungry.

Well, as soon as Horsey and I return to New York, we hasten[16] to Mindy's restaurant on Broadway and relate the bet Horsey makes in Boston, and right away so many citizens, including Mindy himself, wish to take a piece of the proposition that it is oversubscribed by a large sum in no time.

Then Mindy remarks that he does not see Nicely-Nicely Jones for **a month of Sundays**, and then everybody present remembers

12 *unusual*: consider something to be better than it really is
13 *formal*: on
14 *legal*: someone who lies in a court of law, here used to exaggerate
15 129 kg
16 *literary*: go somewhere in a hurry

that they do not see Nicely-Nicely around lately, either, and this leads to a discussion of where Nicely-Nicely can be, although up to this moment if nobody sees Nicely-Nicely but once in the next ten years it will be considered sufficient.

Well, Willie the Worrier, who is a bookmaker by trade, is among those present, and he remembers that the last time he looks for Nicely-Nicely hoping to collect a marker[17] of some years standing, Nicely-Nicely is living at the Rest Hotel in West 49th Street, and nothing will do Horsey but I must go with him over to the Rest to make inquiry for Nicely-Nicely, and there we learn that he leaves a forwarding address away up on Morningside Heights in care of somebody by the name of Slocum.

So Horsey calls a short[18], and away we go to this address, which turns out to be a five-story walk-up apartment, and a card downstairs shows that Slocum lives on the top floor. It takes Horsey and me ten minutes to walk up the five flights as we are by no means accustomed to exercise of this nature, and when we finally reach a door marked Slocum, we are plumb tuckered out, and have to sit down on the top step and rest awhile.

Then I ring the bell at this door marked Slocum, and who appears but a tall young Judy with black hair who is without doubt beautiful, but who is so skinny we have to look twice to see her, and when I ask her if she can give me any information about a party named Nicely-Nicely Jones, she says to me like this:

"I guess you mean Quentin," she says. "Yes," she says, "Quentin is here. Come in, gentlemen."

So we step into an apartment, and as we do so a thin, sickly-looking character gets up out of a chair by the window, and in a weak voice says good evening. It is a good evening, at that, so Horsey and I say good evening right back at him, very polite, and then we stand there waiting for Nicely-Nicely to appear, when the beautiful skinny young Judy says:

"Well," she says, "this is Mr. Quentin Jones."

17 an amount of money that Nicely-Nicely owes him
18 *Runyonese*: a taxi

Then Horsey and I take another **swivel** at the thin character, and we can see that it is nobody but Nicely-Nicely, at that, but the way he changes since we last observe him is practically shocking to us both, because he is undoubtedly all **shrunk** up. In fact, he looks as if he is about half what he is **in his prime**, and his face is pale and thin, and his eyes are away back in his head, and while we both shake hands with him it is some time before either of us is able to speak. Then Horsey finally says:

"Nicely," he says, "can we have a few words with you in private on a very important proposition."

Well, at this, and before Nicely-Nicely can answer aye, yes or no, the beautiful skinny young Judy goes out of the room and slams a door behind her, and Nicely-Nicely says:

"My fiancée, Miss Hilda Slocum," he says. "She is a wonderful character. We are to be married as soon as I lose twenty pounds more. It will take a couple of weeks longer," he says.

"**My goodness gracious**, Nicely," Horsey says. "What do you mean lose twenty pounds more? You are practically **emaciated** now. Are you just out of a sick bed, or what?"

"Why," Nicely-Nicely says, "certainly I am not out of a sick bed. I am never healthier in my life. I am on a diet. I lose eighty-three pounds in two months, and am now down to 200. I feel great," he says. "It is all because of my fiancée, Miss Hilda Slocum. She rescues me from gluttony and obesity, or anyway," Nicely-Nicely says, "this is what Miss Hilda Slocum calls it. My, I feel good. I love Miss Hilda Slocum very much," Nicely-Nicely says. "It is a case of love at first sight on both sides the day we meet in the subway[19]. I am **wedged** in one of the **turnstile** gates, and she kindly pushes on me from behind until I wiggle through. I can see she has a kind heart, so I date her up for a movie that night and propose to her while the newsreel is on. But" Nicely-Nicely says, "Hilda tells me at once that she will never marry a fat slob[20]. She says I must put myself in her hands and she will reduce me by scientific methods and then she will become my ever-loving wife, but not before."

19 *US English*: the underground train in New York
20 *informal*: someone who is lazy or untidy

"So," Nicely-Nicely says "I come to live here with Miss Hilda Slocum and her mother, so she can supervise my diet. Her mother is thinner than Hilda. And I surely feel great," Nicely-Nicely says. "Look," he says.

And with this, he pulls out the waistband of his pants[21], and shows enough spare space to hide War Admiral[22] in, but the effort seems to be a strain on him, and he has to sit down in his chair again.

"My goodness gracious," Horsey says. "What do you eat, Nicely?"

"Well," Nicely-Nicely says, "I eat anything that does not contain **starch**, but," he says, "of course everything worth eating contains starch, so I really do not eat much of anything whatever. My fiancée, Miss Hilda Slocum, arranges my diet. She is an expert dietitian and runs a widely known department on diet in a magazine by the name of Let's Keep House."

Then Horsey tells Nicely-Nicely of how he is matched to eat against this Joel Duffle, of Boston, for a nice side bet, and how he has a forfeit of a thousand dollars already posted for appearance, and how many of Nicely-Nicely's admirers along Broadway are looking to win themselves out of all their troubles by betting on him, and at first Nicely-Nicely listens with great interest, and his eyes are shining like six bits[23], but then he becomes very sad, and says:

"It is no use, gentlemen," he says. "My fiancée, Miss Hilda Slocum, will never hear of me going off my diet even for a little while. Only yesterday I try to talk her into letting me have a little pumpernickel instead of toasted wholewheat bread, and she says if I even think of such a thing again, she will break our engagement. Horsey," he says, "do you ever eat toasted wholewheat bread for a month **running**? Toasted? He says.

"No," Horsey says. "What I eat is nice, white French bread, and corn muffins, and hot biscuits with gravy on them."

21 US English: trousers
22 a famous racehorse of the time
23 US English, old-fashioned: a 'bit' was an old coin worth 12½ cents

"Stop," Nicely-Nicely says. "You are eating yourself into **an early grave**, and, furthermore," he says, "you are breaking my heart. But," he says, "the more I think of my following depending on me in this emergency, the sadder it makes me feel to think I am unable to oblige them. However," he says, "let us call Miss Hilda Slocum in on an outside chance and see what her reactions to your proposition are."

So we call Miss Hilda Slocum in, and Horsey explains our **predicament** in putting so much faith in Nicely-Nicely only to find him dieting, and Miss Hilda Slocum's reactions are to order Horsey and me out of the joint with instructions never to darken her door again[24], and when we are a block away we can still hear her voice speaking very firmly to Nicely-Nicely.

Well, personally, I figure this ends the matter, for I can see that Miss Hilda Slocum is a most determined character, indeed, and the chances are it does end it, at that, if Horsey does not happen to get a wonderful **break**.

He is at Belmont Park one afternoon, and he has a real good thing[25] in a jump race, and when a **brisk** young character in a hard straw hat and eyeglasses comes along and asks him what he likes, Horsey mentions this good thing, figuring he will move himself in for a few dibs if the good thing connects.

Well, it connects all right, and the brisk young character is very grateful to Horsey for his information, and is giving him plenty of much-obliges[26], and nothing else, and Horsey is about to mention that they do not accept much-obliges at his hotel, when the brisk young character mentions that he is nobody but Mr. McBurgle and that he is the editor of the Let's Keep House magazine, and for Horsey to drop in and see him any time he is around that way.

Naturally, Horsey remembers what Nicely-Nicely says about Miss Hilda Slocum working for this Let's Keep House magazine, and he relates the story of the eating contest to Mr. McBurgle and asks him if he will kindly use his influence with Miss Hilda

24 *often humorous*: used for telling someone never to come back to your house again
25 a horse that is very likely to win (or *connect*)
26 if you say 'much obliged' you are thanking someone politely

Slocum to get her to release Nicely-Nicely from his diet long enough for the contest. Then Horsey gives Mr. McBurgle a tip on another winner, and Mr. McBurgle must use plenty of influence on Miss Hilda Slocum at once, as the next day she calls Horsey up at his hotel before he is out of bed, and speaks to him as follows:

"Of course," Miss Hilda Slocum says, "I will never change my attitude about Quentin, but," she says, "I can appreciate that he feels very bad about you gentlemen relying on him and having to disappoint you. He feels that he lets you down, which is by no means true, but it weighs upon his mind. It is interfering with his diet.

"Now," Miss Hilda Slocum says, "I do not approve of your contest, because," she says, "it is **placing a premium on** gluttony, but I have a friend by the name of Miss Violette Shumberger who may answer your purpose. She is my dearest friend from childhood, but it is only because I love her dearly that this friendship endures. She is extremely fond of eating," Miss Slocum says. "In spite of my **pleadings**, and my warnings, and my own example, she persists in food. It is disgusting to me but I finally learn that it is no use arguing with her.

"She remains my dearest friend," Miss Hilda Slocum says, "though she continues her practice of eating, and I am informed that she is **phenomenal** in this respect. In fact," she says, "Nicely-Nicely tells me to say to you that if Miss Violette Shumberger can perform the eating **exploits** I relate to him from **hearsay** she is a lily[27]. Goodbye," Miss Hilda Slocum says. "You cannot have Nicely-Nicely."

Well, nobody cares much about this idea of a stand-in for Nicely-Nicely in such a situation, and especially a Judy that no one ever hears of before, and many citizens are in favor of pulling out of the contest altogether. But Horsey has his thousand-dollar forfeit to think of, and as no one can suggest anyone else, he finally arranges a personal meet with the Judy suggested by Miss Hilda Slocum.

27 *Runyonese*: a good thing, a winner

He comes into Mindy's one evening with a female character who is so fat it is necessary to push three tables together to give her room for her lap, and it seems that this character is Miss Violette Shumberger. She weighs maybe 250 pounds[28], but she is by no means an old Judy, and by no means bad-looking. She has a face the size of a town clock and enough chins for a fire escape, but she has a nice smile, and pretty teeth, and a laugh that is so **hearty** it knocks the whipped cream off an order of strawberry shortcake on a table fifty feet away and arouses the **indignation** of a customer by the name of Goldstein who is about to consume same.

Well, Horsey's idea in bringing her into Mindy's is to get some kind of line on her eating form, and she is clocked by many experts when she starts putting on the hot meat, and it is agreed by one and all that she is by no means a selling-plater[29]. In fact, by the time she gets through, even Mindy admits she has plenty of class, and the **upshot** of it all is Miss Violette Shumberger is chosen to eat against Joel Duffle.

Maybe you hear something of this great eating contest that comes off in New York one night in the early summer of 1937. Of course eating contests are by no means anything new, and in fact they are quite an old-fashioned pastime in some sections of this country, such as the South and East, but this is the first big public contest of the kind in years, and it creates no little comment along Broadway.

In fact, there is some mention of it in the blats[30], and it is not a **frivolous** proposition in any respect, and more dough is wagered on it than any other eating contest in history, with Joel Duffle a 6 to 5 favorite over Miss Violette Shumberger all the way through.

This Joel Duffle comes to New York several days before the contest with the character by the name of Conway, and requests a meet with Miss Violette Shumberger to agree on the final details and who shows up with Miss Violette Shumberger as her

28 113 kg
29 in horseracing, a horse that is not good enough to compete in normal races
30 *Runyonese*: the newspapers

coach and adviser but Nicely-Nicely Jones. He is even thinner and more peaked-looking[31] than when Horsey and I see him last, but he says he feels great, and that he is within six pounds of his marriage to Miss Hilda Slocum.

Well, it seems that his presence is really due to Miss Hilda Slocum herself, because she says that after getting her dearest friend Miss Violette Shumberger into this **jack pot**, it is only fair to do all she can to help her win it, and the only way she can think of is to let Nicely-Nicely give Violette the benefit of his experience and advice.

But afterward we learn that what really happens is that this editor, Mr. McBurgle, gets greatly interested in the contest, and when he discovers that in spite of his influence, Miss Hilda Slocum declines to permit Nicely-Nicely to personally compete, but puts in a pinch eater[32], he is quite indignant and insists on her letting Nicely-Nicely **school** Violette.

Furthermore we afterward learn that when Nicely-Nicely returns to the apartment on Morningside Heights after giving Violette a lesson, Miss Hilda Slocum always smells his breath to see if he **indulges** in any food during his absence.

Well, this Joel Duffle is a tall character with stooped shoulders, and a sad expression, and he does not look as if he can eat his way out of a tea shoppe[33], but as soon as he commences to discuss the details of the contest, anybody can see that he knows what time it is[34] in situations such as this. In fact, Nicely-Nicely says he can tell at once from the way Joel Duffle talks that he is a dangerous opponent, and he says while Miss Violette Shumberger impresses him as an improving eater, he is only sorry she does not have more seasoning[35].

This Joel Duffle suggests that the contest consist of twelve courses of strictly American food, each side to be allowed to

31 US English (British English 'peaky'): pale and not healthy in appearance
32 sport: in baseball, a pinch player is a substitute player
33 a small restaurant that serves tea, cakes and sandwiches (an old-fashioned spelling of 'shop')
34 slang: know a lot about a certain situation
35 if you are seasoned, you are experienced. Seasoning is also salt, pepper or other spices added to food to improve the taste. Here the writer is playing with the word.

pick six dishes, doing the picking in rotation, and specifying the weight and quantity of the course selected to any amount the contestant making the pick desires, and each course is to be divided for eating exactly in half, and after Miss Violette Shumberger and Nicely-Nicely whisper together a while, they say the terms are quite satisfactory.

Then Horsey tosses a coin for the first pick, and Joel Duffle says heads, and it is heads, and he chooses, as the first course, two quarts of ripe olives, twelve bunches of celery, and four pounds of shelled nuts, all this to be split fifty-fifty between them. Miss Violette Shumberger names twelve dozen cherrystone clams as the second course, and Joel Duffle says two gallons of Philadelphia pepperpot soup as the third.

Well, Miss Violette Shumberger and Nicely-Nicely whisper together again, and Violette puts in two five-pound striped bass[36], the heads and tails not to count in the eating, and Joel Duffle names a twenty-two-pound roast turkey. Each vegetable is rated as one course, and Miss Violette Shumberger asks for twelve pounds of mashed potatoes with brown gravy. Joel Duffle says two dozen ears of corn on the cob, and Violette replies with two quarts of lima beans. Joel Duffle calls for twelve bunches of asparagus cooked in butter, and Violette mentions ten pounds of stewed new peas.

This gets them down to the salad, and it is Joel Duffle's play, so he says six pounds of mixed green salad with vinegar and oil **dressing**, and now Miss Violette Shumberger has the final selection, which is the dessert. She says it is a pumpkin pie, two feet across, and not less than three inches deep.

It is agreed that they must eat with knife, fork or spoon, but speed is not to count, and there is to be no time limit, except they cannot pause more than two consecutive minutes at any stage, except in case of **hiccoughs**. They can drink anything, and as much as they please, but liquids are not to count in the scoring. The decision is to be strictly on amount of food consumed, and the judges are to take account of anything left on the plates after a course, but not of loose chewings on bosom

36 a fish

or vest up to an ounce[37]. The losing side is to pay for the food, and in case of a tie they are to eat it off immediately on ham and eggs only.

Well, the scene of this contest is the second-floor dining room of Mindy's restaurant, which is closed to the general public for the occasion, and only parties immediately concerned in the contest are admitted. The contestants are seated on either side of a big table in the center of the room, and each contestant has three waiters.

No talking, and no **rooting** from the spectators is permitted, but of course in any eating contest the principals may speak to each other if they wish, though smart eaters never wish to do this, as talking only wastes energy, and about all they ever say to each is other is please pass the mustard.

About fifty characters from Boston are present to witness the contest, and the same number of citizens of New York are admitted, and among them is this editor, Mr. McBurgle, and he is around asking Horsey if he thinks Miss Violette Shumberger is as good a thing as the jumper at the race track.

Nicely-Nicely arrives on the scene quite early, and his appearance is really most **distressing** to his old friends and admirers, as by this time he is shy[38] so much weight that he is a **pitiful** scene, to be sure, but he tells Horsey and me that he thinks Miss Violette Shumberger has a good chance.

"Of course," he says, "she is **green**. She does not know how to pace herself in competition. But," he says, "she has a wonderful style. I love to watch her eat. She likes the same things I do in the days when I am eating. She is a wonderful character, too. Do you ever notice her smile?" Nicely-Nicely says.

"But," he says, "she is the dearest friend of my fiancée, Miss Hilda Slocum, so let us not speak of this. I try to get Hilda to come to see the contest, but she says it is **repulsive**. Well, anyway" Nicely-Nicely says, "I manage to borrow a few dibs, and am wagering on Miss Violette Shumberger. By the way," he says, "if you happen to think of it, notice her smile."

37 small pieces of food that drop from their mouths that do not weigh very much
38 US English, normally 'shy of something': having less of something than you need

Well, Nicely-Nicely takes a chair about ten feet behind Miss Violette Shumberger, which is as close as the judges will allow him, and he is warned by them that no coaching from the corners will be permitted, but of course Nicely-Nicely knows this rule as well as they do, and furthermore by this time his exertions seem to have left him without any more energy.

There are three judges, and they are all from neutral territory. One of these judges is a party from Baltimore, Maryland, by the name of Packard, who runs a restaurant, and another is a party from Providence, Rhode Island, by the name of Croppers, who is a sausage manufacturer. The third judge is an old Judy by the name of Mrs. Rhubarb, who comes from Philadelphia, and once keeps an actors' boardinghouse[39], and is considered an excellent judge of eaters.

Well, Mindy is the official starter, and at 8:30pm sharp, when there is still much betting among the spectators, he outs with his watch, and says like this:

"Are you ready, Boston? Are you ready, New York?"

Miss Violette Shumberger and Joel Duffle both nod their heads, and Mindy says commence, and the contest is on, with Joel Duffle getting the jump at once on the celery and olives and nuts.

It is apparent that this Joel Duffle is one of these rough-and-tumble eaters that you can hear quite a distance off, especially on clams and soups. He is also an eyebrow eater, an eater whose eyebrows go up as high as the part[40] in his hair as he eats, and this type of eater is undoubtedly very efficient.

In fact, the way Joel Duffle goes through the groceries down to the turkey causes the Broadway spectators some **uneasiness**, and they are whispering to each other that they only wish the old Nicely-Nicely is in there. But personally, I like the way Miss Violette Shumberger eats without undue excitement, and with great **zest**. She cannot keep close to Joel Duffle in the matter of

39 *old-fashioned*: a house in which people pay to live as guests with the family who owns it

40 *US English, (British English,* 'parting'): a line on your head made by combing your hair in two different directions.

speed in the early stages of the contest, as she seems to enjoy chewing her food, but I observe that as it goes along she pulls up on him, and I figure this is not because she is stepping up her pace, but because he is slowing down

When the turkey finally comes on, and is split in two halves right down the middle, Miss Violette Shumberger looks greatly disappointed, and she speaks for the first time as follows:

"Why," she says, "where is the stuffing?"

Well, it seems that nobody mentions any stuffing for the turkey to the chef, so he does not make any stuffing, and Miss Violette Shumberger's disappointment is so plain to be seen that the confidence of the Boston characters is somewhat shaken. They can see that a Judy who can pack away as much fodder as Miss Violette Shumberger has to date, and then beef[41] for stuffing, is really quite an eater.

In fact, Joel Duffle looks quite **startled** when he observes Miss Violette Shumberger's disappointment, and he gazes at her with great respect as she disposes of her share of the turkey, and the mashed potatoes, and one thing and another in such a manner that she moves up on the pumpkin pie on dead even terms with him. In fact, there is little to choose between them at this point, although the judge from Baltimore is calling the attention of the other judges to a turkey leg that he claims Miss Violette Shumberger does not clean as neatly as Joel Duffle does his, but the other judges dismiss this as a technicality.

Then the waiters bring on the pumpkin pie, and it is without doubt quite a large pie, and in fact it is about the size of a **manhole** cover, and I can see that Joel Duffle is observing this pie with a strange expression on his face, although to tell the truth I do not care for the expression on Miss Violette Shumberger's face either.

Well, the pie is cut in two dead center and one half is placed before Miss Violette Shumberger, and the other half before Joel Duffle, and he does not take more than two bites before I see him loosen his **waistband** and take a big swig of water, and thinks I to myself, he is now down to a slow walk, and the pie will decide

41 *informal*: complain

the whole heat, and I am only wishing I am able to wager a little more dough on Miss Violette Shumberger. But about this moment, and before she as much as touches her pie, all of a sudden Violette turns her head and motions to Nicely-Nicely to approach her, and as he approaches, she whispers in his ear.

Now at this, the Boston character by the name of Conway jumps up and claims a foul, and several other Boston characters join him in this claim, and so does Joel Duffle, although afterwards even the Boston characters admit that Joel Duffle is no gentleman to make such a claim against a lady.

Well, there is some confusion over this, and the judges hold a conference, and they rule that there is certainly no foul in the actual eating that they can see, because Miss Violette Shumberger does not touch her pie so far.

But they say that whether it is a foul otherwise all depends on whether Miss Violette Shumberger is requesting advice on the contest from Nicely-Nicely and the judge from Providence, R.I., wishes to know if Nicely-Nicely will kindly relate[42] what passes between him and Violette so they may make a decision.

"Why," Nicely-Nicely says, "all she asks me is can I get her another piece of pie when she finishes the one in front of her."

Now at this, Joel Duffle throws down his knife, and pushes back his plate with all but two bites of his pie left on it, and says to the Boston characters like this:

"Gentlemen," he says, "I am licked. I cannot eat another mouthful. You must admit I put up a game battle, but," he says, "it is useless for me to go on against this Judy who is asking for more pie before she even starts on what is before her. I am almost dying as it is, and I do not wish to destroy myself in a hopeless effort. Gentlemen," he says, "she is not human."

Well, of course this amounts to throwing in the old napkin[43] and Nicely-Nicely stands up on his chair, and says:

"Three cheers for Miss Violette Shumberger!"

42 *formal*: tell someone about something that has happened or what someone has said
43 usually **throw in the towel** (means 'give up', see page 159). Here, napkin is used instead of towel. A napkin is a piece of cloth or paper used for protecting your clothes and wiping your mouth and hands while you are eating.

Then Nicely-Nicely gives the first cheer in person, but the effort **overtaxes** his strength, and he falls off the chair in a **faint** just as Joel Duffle collapses under the table, and the doctors at the Clinic Hospital are greatly **baffled** to receive, from the same address at the same time, one patient who is suffering from undernourishment, and another patient who is unconscious from overeating.

Well, in the meantime, after the excitement subsides, and wagers are settled, we take Miss Violette Shumberger to the main floor in Mindy's for a midnight snack, and when she speaks of her wonderful triumph, she is disposed[44] to give much credit to Nicely-Nicely Jones.

"You see," Violette says, "what I really whisper to him is that I am a goner. I whisper to him that I cannot possibly take one bite of the pie if my life depends on it, and if he has any bets down to try and hedge them off as quickly as possible.

"I fear," she says, "that Nicely-Nicely will be greatly disappointed in my showing, but I have a confession to make to him when he gets out of hospital. I forget about the contest," Violette says, "and eat my regular dinner of pig's knuckles and sauerkraut an hour before the contest starts, and," she says, "I have no doubt this tends to affect my form somewhat. So, "she says, "I owe everything to Nicely-Nicely's quick thinking."

It is several weeks after the great eating contest that I run into Miss Hilda Slocum on Broadway, and it seems to me that she looks much better nourished than the last time I see her, and when I mention this she says:

"Yes," she says, "I cease dieting. I learn my lesson," she says. "I learn that male characters do not appreciate anybody who tries to ward off surplus tissue[45]. What male characters wish is **substance**. Why," she says, "only a week ago my editor, Mr. McBurgle, tells me he will love to take me dancing if only I get something on me for him to take hold of. I am very fond of dancing," she says.

---

44 *formal*: be willing to do something
45 men do not appreciate women who try to stay slim

"But," I say, "what of Nicely-Nicely Jones? I do not see him around lately."

"Why," Miss Hilda Slocum says, "do you not hear what this cad does? Why, as soon as he is strong enough to leave the hospital, he elopes[46] with my dearest friend, Miss Violette Shumberger, leaving me a note saying something about two souls with but a single thought. They are down in Florida running a barbecue stand, and," she says, "the chances are, eating like seven mules."

"Miss Slocum," I say, "can I interest you in a portion of Mindy's chicken fricassee?"

"With dumplings?" Miss Hilda Slocum says. "Yes," she says, "you can. Afterwards I have a date to go dancing with Mr. McBurgle. I am crazy about dancing," she says.

---

46 *old-fashioned*: if two people elope, they go away secretly to get married

Post-reading activities

Understanding the story

Use these questions to help you check that you have understood the story.

Before the contest

1 What is the storyteller doing at the beginning of the story?
2 What is Horse Thief's best quality, according to the storyteller?
3 Why does Horse Thief interrupt the men at the next table?
4 How does Horse Thief prove that his proposal is a serious one?
5 Why is Horse Thief so confident when he makes the bet?
6 What details about the contest do the men agree on?
7 Why is it difficult to find Nicely-Nicely?
8 What stops Nicely-Nicely from competing?
9 Other than losing weight, what effect does Nicely-Nicely's diet have on him?
10 How does Horse Thief try to persuade Nicely-Nicely to compete?
11 Why does Nicely-Nicely say: 'You are breaking my heart'?
12 Why does Mr McBurgle want to help Horse Thief? How does he help?
13 What is Miss Slocum's relationship to Miss Shumberger? What complicates their relationship?
14 What is Horse Thief and the storyteller's impression of Miss Shumberger?
15 Whose decision is it to make Nicely-Nicely Miss Shumberger's coach?
16 What makes Nicely-Nicely realize that Joel Duffle is going to be hard to beat?

The contest

17 Draw a plan of the seating arrangement in Mindy's restaurant to show where all the characters are.
18 What is different about the eating styles of the contestants?
19 What is the effect of Miss Shumberger asking for stuffing?
20 What does Miss Shumberger say to Nicely-Nicely?
21 How does she win the contest if she doesn't eat the pie?
22 Why are the doctors at the hospital confused?
23 What do they do after the contest?
24 What mistake did Miss Shumberger make before the contest?
25 When the storyteller meets Miss Slocum again, what has changed?

Language study

Grammar

Narrative tenses

The story is told using a very limited range of tenses. Tenses are used in language to make meaning clearer; one question about this way of writing is therefore how easy it is to understand.

1 **Read the extracts below and the two statements for each one. Which statement is true, a) or b)?**

1 *Professor D. is a professor in a college out West before he turns to playing the horses for a livelihood.* (page 164)
a) Professor D. is mainly a professor but he also bets on horses.
b) Professor D. was a professor before he gave it up to bet on horses.

2 *Mindy remarks that he does not see Nicely-Nicely Jones for a month of Sundays.* (page 165)
a) Mindy hasn't seen Nicely-Nicely for a long time. This is unusual.
b) Mindy often goes without seeing Nicely-Nicely for long periods of time.

3 *I figure this ends the matter, and the chances are it does end it, at that, if Horsey does not happen to get a wonderful break.* (page 169)
a) The storyteller thinks that it is likely that this will end the matter unless Horsey has a wonderful break.
b) The storyteller thinks that this would probably have ended the matter if Horsey had not had a wonderful break.

4 *Mr. McBurgle must use plenty of influence on Miss Hilda Slocum at once, as the next day she calls Horsey up at his hotel.* (page 170)
a) It is necessary for Mr. McBurgle to use his influence on Miss Slocum if she is to call Horsey at his hotel.
b) Mr. McBurgle must have used his influence on her because she called Horsey at his hotel.

5 *She likes the same things I do in the days when I am eating.* (page 174)
a) Miss Shumberger likes the same food Nicely-Nicely did when he was eating and not on a diet.
b) She likes the same food Nicely-Nicely likes on the special days when he is allowed to eat.

2 **Look back at your answers in exercise 1 and find examples of the following verb forms:**

a) the past simple (e.g. *She did*)
b) a past modal structure (e.g. *She might have done*)
c) the third conditional (e.g. *She would have done ...if ...*)
d) the continuous aspect (e.g. *She was doing*)
e) the perfect aspect (e.g. *She has done*)

3 **Match each verb form in exercise 2 with its function (1–5).**

1 used to describe events and actions that are in progress over a period of time
2 used to speculate about events and actions that happened before now
3 used to describe events and actions that happened before now
4 used to describe events and actions that happened at some indefinite point between a point in the past and now
5 used to imagine what didn't happen but would have done in different circumstances

4 **Rewrite the verbs in bold using one of the verb forms described in exercises 2 and 3, depending on their meaning.**

1 *Horse Thief is not called by this name because he **ever steals** a horse but because it is the consensus of public opinion that he may steal one.*
2 *He is without doubt the greatest eater alive. He **just wins** a unique wager.*
3 *I **do not say** that Nicely-Nicely is the greatest eater in all history.*
4 *But afterward we **learn** that what really **happens is** that this editor, Mr. McBurgle, **gets** greatly interested in the contest.*
5 *I have a confession to make to him when he gets out of hospital. I **forget** about the contest.*

Verb patterns

Many words and phrases in English can be followed by a verb. Here are two examples from the story:

*Boston characters are always **ready to visit** New York.*

*Many citizens are **in favor of pulling out** of the contest altogether*

Notice that *ready* is followed by the infinitive with *to*, but *in favour of* is followed by the *-ing* form of the verb. (*Favor* is the US English spelling)

5 **Match the verb structures in bold in the extracts (1–11) with the rules (a–e).**

1 *Characters such as these are **bound to be** politicians, retired cops, or contractors.*

2 *I can produce a character who will out eat your party for ten thousand, and as much more as you **care to put up**.*

3 *I am **prepared to wager** all the money I can possibly raise.*

4 *My fiancée will never **hear of me going off** my diet even for a little while.*

5 *Yesterday I try to **talk her into letting** me have a little pumpernickel.*

6 *The chances are it does end it, at that, if Horsey does not **happen to get** a wonderful break.*

7 *It is disgusting to me but it is **no use arguing** with her.*

8 *... a customer who is **about to consume** some strawberry shortcake.*

9 *Mr. McBurgle **insists on her letting** Nicely-Nicely school Violette.*

10 *I am almost dying as it is, and I do not **wish to destroy** myself in a hopeless effort.*

11 *I am very **fond of dancing**.*

a) adjective + *to* + infinitive e.g. ***ready to visit***
b) preposition + *-ing* e.g. ***in favour of pulling out***
c) verb + *to* + infinitive
d) verb + preposition + someone/something + *-ing*
e) noun + *-ing*

Some other verbs that are followed by the infinitive with *to* include:

decide   intend   agree   promise   refuse   want

Verbs that are following by *-ing* include:

consider   enjoy   imagine   keep   mind   miss

A good dictionary will show you which pattern to use. Look at the example sentences provided to see how a word is used:

---

decide verb
  1 make a choice about what you are going to do; **decide to do something:** *He decided to stay and see what would happen.*

---

6 **Complete the sentences with the verbs in brackets in the correct form, either infinitive with *to* or the *-ing* form.**

1 Anita is fond of .... (*play*) the piano.

2 I happened .... (*meet*) an old friend in town the other day.

3 I talked her into .... (go) to London with me.
4 I told him he didn't need a hotel, but he wouldn't hear of
   .... (stay) with us.
5 I want to congratulate you on .... (win) the contest so
   convincingly.
6 I warned them against .... (use) this computer.
7 I was about .... (get) undressed when there was a knock
   on the door.
8 If you have problems at home, it is bound .... (affect)
   your work.
9 It's no use .... (ask) me. I don't know.
10 Just imagine .... (sit) behind your big new desk in your
   own office!
11 Peter wished he'd never promised .... (help) them.
12 Since moving abroad, she misses .... (see) her friends.
13 The Prime Minister said he did not wish .... (comment)
   at the present time.
14 You can see a doctor today, if you are prepared ....
   (wait).

Literary analysis

Plot

1 Write your own one-sentence summary of the plot.
2 Horse Thief's plan is simple: he will put Nicely-Nicely up against
  Joel Duffle, Nicely-Nicely will win and he will make a lot of money.
  What are the surprises that 1) upset his plan and 2) make it right
  again?
3 Could Joel Duffle have won? How?
4 Do you think Nicely-Nicely and Miss Shumberger cheated?
5 How does the contest affect the lives of the people involved?
6 Do you think the story has a message? If so, what is the message?
  And is it serious or humorous?

The role of food in the story

7 In the other stories in this collection, food and eating are associated
  with the home and families. Where is the food in this story eaten?
  What does this suggest about the characters in the story?
8 Make a list of some of the meals that you remember from the story.
  How would you describe the food in general?

9 What is the storyteller's attitude to eating? How do you know? What is his attitude to dieting?
10 How is the eating contest meal similar to a normal meal in a restaurant? How is it different?
11 'A piece of *the* pie' is an expression that means 'a share of something'. How does this saying relate to the events in the story?

Character

12 What do you know about the storyteller? What kind of person is he?
13 Which characters are described physically? Why is their appearance important?
14 What do Horse Thief, Nicely-Nicely and the narrator do for a living? Where does their money come from?
15 How are the men's names different from the women's names?
16 The two women in the story are friends. How are they different from one another? Which do you like more? Why?

Narration

17 Read the opening paragraph of the story again. It consists of an extract from later in the story (the first sentence) and a one-sentence summary of the story (the second sentence). Could this paragraph be cut from the story? What effect would that have?
18 Why is the storyteller in a good position to tell the story?
19 To what extent does the storyteller take part in the action of the story? Is he simply a witness to the events or does he contribute to them in some way?
20 How would the story be different if the story had been told from the point of view of Nicely-Nicely or Miss Shumberger?

Style

The use of the present tense to tell jokes, anecdotes and other personal stories is very common in everyday speech. When the present tense is used this way it is called the 'historical' or 'narrative' present. A *Piece of Pie* uses the narrative present throughout.

21 Compare two versions of the same extract from the story. What is the effect of using the narrative present?

Narrative past:

> And with this, Horsey outed with a bundle of coarse notes and tossed it on the table, and right away one of the Boston characters slapped his hand on the money and said:
>
> "Bet."

Narrative present:

> And with this, Horsey outs with a bundle of coarse notes and tosses it on the table, and right away one of the Boston characters slaps his hand on the money and says:
>
> "Bet."

22 Look at the beginnings of the paragraphs in the story. What word most commonly introduces the paragraphs? What effect does this have?

23 Read the second paragraph again, which introduces Horse Thief and the storyteller. What is the difference in the style of language in the first part of the paragraph ('joint', 'slaps a lip over') and the second part ('partaking', 'a character')?

24 Do you think this mix of styles suggests:
   a) that the characters enjoy playing with language and find it funny to pretend to sound important,
   b) that they think that they are important but do not realize that they sound silly, or
   c) neither of the above? Why?

Hyperbole and understatement

Sometimes the writer uses hyperbole, which is a way of emphasizing what you are saying by describing it as far more extreme than it really is:

> He pulls out the waistband of his pants, and shows enough spare space to hide War Admiral in.

At other times, understatement is used, where something is made to sound smaller or less important than it really is:

> Miss Hilda Slocum's reactions are to order Horsey and me out of the joint, and when we are a block away we can still hear her voice speaking very firmly to Nicely-Nicely.

If you are a block away from a five-storey apartment, it should be impossible to hear someone 'speaking firmly'. She must be shouting at him very loudly.

25 Do the following extracts contain examples of hyperbole or
    understatement?
    a) *I can see that Miss Hilda Slocum is a most determined character.*
    b) *She has a face the size of a town clock and enough chins for a fire
       escape*
    c) *She has a laugh that is so hearty it knocks the whipped cream off an
       order of strawberry shortcake on a table fifty feet away.*
    d) *This is the first big public contest of the kind in years, and it creates
       no little comment along Broadway.*
    e) *They can see that a Judy who can pack away as much fodder as Miss
       Violette Shumberger is really quite an eater.*

26 What is the effect of these techniques?

*Guidance to the above literary terms, answer keys to all the exercises and
activities, plus a wealth of other reading-practice material, can be found at:
www.macmillanenglish.com/readers.*

Recipes

Roast turkey with stuffing

From *An Old-Fashioned Thanksgiving*

As well as Thanksgiving, turkey is also a popular meal at Christmas in many countries. Serves 4–6 people.

For the stuffing:

- 6 slices of old bread, cut into small cubes
- 100 g butter
- 1 onion, finely chopped
- 3 tsp[1] herbs: sage, thyme, summer savory, marjoram (use any combination)
- salt and pepper

For the turkey:

- 1 turkey of about 4 kg
- 100 g butter
- 1 litre chicken stock

Heat the oven to 220°C. Mix all the stuffing ingredients in a bowl. Keep mixing, slowly adding boiling water until it has been absorbed and you can pick up the mixture in wet balls. Clean the turkey inside and out with water. Fill the hole at the neck end with the stuffing and place the rest in the middle of the turkey. Put the turkey in a deep roasting dish. Rub the outside with the butter and salt and pepper. Pour the chicken stock into the roasting dish around the turkey.

Roast the turkey in the middle of the oven for 30 minutes. Reduce the oven temperature to 170°C and continue roasting for about 3 more hours, or longer for a larger turkey. Baste the turkey every 20 minutes. It is cooked when you push a knife deep into the turkey and the juices that come out are clear (not pink). Transfer the turkey to a cutting board and keep the juices from the pan. Take out the stuffing and put it on a serving dish. Keep the stuffing warm in the oven while the turkey rests out of the oven for 30 minutes covered with aluminium foil. Cut up the turkey in slices and serve it with the stuffing, roasted potatoes, boiled vegetables and gravy.

1 tsp = teaspoon, tbsp = tablespoon

Little pies (*Les petits pâtés*)

From *The Little Pies*

This recipe is based on pies from the town of Pézenas in the south of France, near Nîmes. Eat them as a starter or just have them for a snack. Makes 6 pies.

- 300 g minced lamb (should have the fat on it)
- ½ tsp nutmeg
- ½ tsp cumin
- ½ tsp cinnamon
- 1 tsp brown sugar
- salt and pepper to taste
- 300 g shortcrust pastry (home-made or shop-bought)
- 1 egg (beaten with a fork)

Heat the oven to 200°C. Mix the lamb, spices, sugar, salt and pepper together in a bowl with a fork. Throw a little flour over a surface and roll out the pastry until it is just 3–5 mm thick. Cut out 6 circles about 12 cm in diameter. Put a tablespoon of the mixture in the middle of each circle, brush the edges of the pastry with water, then fold over the circle to make a semi-circle or half-moon shape. Push the edges together with your fingers to close the pastry so that none of the mixture will come out.

Brush some egg over each pie and then put them in the oven for 20 minutes. Serve with salad or eat them on their own.

Australian barbecued steak with sauce

From A Piece of Steak

Australians are famous for their love of barbecues. This delicious sauce tastes good with any meat and is a classic 'Aussie' accompaniment.

For the steak:

- 4 steaks, each approximately 2.5 cm thick
- olive oil and seasoning (salt and pepper)

For the barbecue sauce:

- 800 ml tomato sauce
- 3 tbsp treacle
- 3 tbsp tomato purée
- 2 tbsp white wine vinegar
- 1 tbsp mustard
- 1 clove garlic, crushed
- 2 tbsp sweet chilli sauce
- 1 tsp oregano
- 1 tbsp Worcester sauce
- 1 tsp 'Vegemite' (a yeast-based paste, called 'Marmite' in the UK. This classic Australian ingredient is optional for the sauce – it will taste just as good without it.)

To make the barbecue sauce, mix all the ingredients in a small saucepan. Heat it gently for 20 minutes until it becomes thick. Pour the sauce into a sterilized bottle. You can store it in the fridge for up to three weeks.

Brush both sides of the steaks with olive oil. Heat the barbecue until the charcoal turns white. Season one side of the steaks with salt and pepper, then place them on the grill seasoned-side down. Leave them to cook for the desired time (see cooking times below) and turn them once. Place the steaks on a plate and serve with the barbecue sauce.

Approximate cooking times:

'Rare' 2–3 minutes on each side. The meat is red inside.

'Medium' 3–4 minutes on each side. There is a thin line of red in the middle.

'Well done' 5–6 minutes on each side. The meat is brown inside.

Christmas rolls *(Bocadillos de Navidad)*

From *Like Water for Chocolate*

These rolls are eaten in Mexico on 24th December, but, despite their name, they can be eaten at any time of year. This makes enough filling for 4 rolls.

- ½ chorizo sausage for cooking (or any spicy sausage of your choice)
- ½ onion, finely chopped
- 90 g tin sardines
- 90 g tin serrano chillies, finely chopped (just one or two chillies if you don't like it too spicy, or a less spicy variety of chilli)
- pinch of oregano
- pinch of salt
- 4 hard bread rolls

Break up the sausage into small pieces and fry it over a low heat, making sure that it does not get too brown. Don't use much oil because chorizo sausage is greasy already. Debone the sardines and gently scrape off the skin with a knife. Remove the sausage from the heat and mix it with the onions, sardines, chillies and oregano. Let the mixture stand to cool. Cut the rolls open, fill them with a generous amount of the mixture, then cover them with a cloth. Leave them for a few hours, overnight if possible, for the bread to absorb the grease from the mixture. Bake in a warm oven (170°C) for 10 minutes. Serve hot.

Pumpkin pie

From *A Piece of Pie*

This rich, heavy dessert is perfect for big groups of hungry people. The sweetness of the pumpkin is emphasized by the other sweet ingredients and the spices give it the taste of winter.

- 500 g shortcrust pastry (home-made or shop-bought)
- a small pumpkin (or medium-sized squash) of about 2 kg
- 100 ml maple syrup
- 2 tbsp sugar
- 1 tsp ground cinnamon
- 1 tsp ground ginger
- ½ tsp freshly grated nutmeg
- ½ tsp salt
- 1 tsp vanilla extract
- 2 large eggs plus 1 yolk, beaten
- 150 ml evaporated milk

Heat the oven to 200°C. Cut the pumpkin in half and take out the seeds and soft fibres. Put it in a roasting dish with the sides you have cut at the bottom. Pour 2 tablespoons of water into the dish and roast for an hour, until it is soft. Leave it to cool, then use a large spoon to take out the pumpkin flesh. Put it in a food processor. Mix it until you have a smooth texture, or purée, then strain out the liquid by putting it in a sieve and leaving it for an hour.

Meanwhile prepare the pastry. Throw a little flour over a surface and roll out the pastry until it is 5 mm thick and use it to line a 22 cm pie tin with a removable bottom. Put it in the fridge for 15 minutes. Cover the pastry with baking paper and some heavy objects such as dried beans. Bake in the oven for 15 minutes. Remove the heavy objects and paper, and cook for 5–10 minutes more until the pastry is light gold in colour. Remove it from the oven. Turn the oven temperature down to 180°C.

Put 400 g of pumpkin puree in a large bowl. Stir in the maple syrup, sugar, vanilla extract, salt and spices. Mix in the eggs then gradually stir in the evaporated milk until the consistency is thick and creamy. Pour the filling into your pasty case and bake for 30–40 minutes, until the filling is solid but slightly wobbly in the centre. Remove the pie from the oven and leave it to cool on a wire rack. Cut into slices and serve with cream.

Essay questions

Language analysis

> Discuss how one of the language areas you've studied contributes to the telling of two OR MORE of the stories in the collection.

Analysing the question

What is the question asking?

It is asking you to:
- choose one language area from the index on page 205
- explain how this language area functions in the context of storytelling in this collection
- use extracts from two or more of the stories in the collection as examples.

Preparing your answer

1 Look back through the *Language analysis* sections of the stories you've read and choose a language area that you feel confident about.

2 Make notes about the language area. Include notes on form and use.

3 Choose examples from two stories. If possible, choose extracts from different periods.

4 Look back at the question and your notes and plan your essay. Here is an example of an essay plan:

Introduction	Introduce the area you are going to describe.
Main body 1	Explain the general function of the area you have chosen. Use examples from more than one story.
Main body 2	Analyze how the area contributes to the style, narrative or atmosphere of the stories, referring to specific passages in the stories.
Conclusion	Summarize the literary use and function of the language area you focused on.

Literary analysis

Choose two stories from this collection. Compare and contrast what the food in the stories tells us about the characters. Consider the characters' attitude to food, the type of food they cook and eat and their lifestyles.

Analysing the question

What is the question asking?

It is asking you to:
– look at two stories in the collection
– outline the characters' relationships with food
– draw conclusions about the characters from the food in the stories and their relationship to it
– describe any similarities and differences between the two stories.

Preparing your answer

1 Choose two stories whose characters interest you.
2 Make notes about the nature of the food in the story: what type of food it is; who prepares and eats it; what it represents; how the characters feel about it, and so on.
3 Find key scenes in the stories where food is mentioned in relation to one or more characters. Note any useful quotations.
4 Make a list of similarities and differences between the stories in regard to the food and characters in each one.
5 Read the question again and write an essay plan, e.g.

Introduction	Briefly introduce the two stories
Story 1	Describe the food in the first story and what it tells us about one or more characters.
Story 2	Describe the food in the second story and what it tells us about the main characters.
Similarities	Compare the two stories in regard to food and characterization. What do they have in common?
Differences	Contrast the two stories in this regard.
Conclusion	Make a general comment about the importance of food in the portrayal of the characters in both stories.

Glossary

The definitions in the glossary refer to the meanings of the words and phrases as they are used in the short stories in this collection. Some words and phrases may also have other meanings which are not given here. The definitions are arranged in the story in which they appear, and in alphabetical order.

An Old-Fashioned Thanksgiving

air (n) a feeling or attitude that someone has

array (n) a large group of people or things arranged to look impressive

at hand PHRASE going to happen soon

audacity (n) the confidence to say or do what you want

awe-stricken (adj) (usually **awestruck**) feeling extremely impressed by something

banish (v) officially order someone to leave a place or country as a punishment

batch (n) an amount of a food that is prepared or baked at one time

beam (v) smile in a very obvious way

bent on PHRASE very determined to achieve something

bitter (adj) something that is bitter has a strong, sharp taste that is not sweet

bob (v) move up and down, especially on water

break in (past **broke**) PHRASAL VERB interrupt when someone is talking

burn (v) if you burn to do something, you feel a very strong wish or need to do something

bustle (v) do something or go somewhere quickly, usually because you are very busy

chivalry (n) the qualities of being brave and honourable, defending the weak, originally used to talk about knights

cloak (n) a long, loose coat without sleeves, that fastens around your neck

crestfallen (adj) sad and disappointed, especially when something has not succeeded

earthen (adj) made of clay

errand (n) a small job that involves going to collect or deliver something

flock (n) normally a group of birds, sheep or goats, here used to describe the family

flounder (v) move with great difficulty and in an uncontrolled way

flushed (adj) red in the face because you are hot and working hard

formidable (adj) very impressive in size and strength

fowl (n) a bird that is kept on a farm for its eggs and meat, for example a chicken or a duck

fray (n) a fight or argument

genteel (adj) typical of polite, well-educated people belonging to a high social class who have strict moral standards

glance (n) a quick look at someone or something

goblin (n) a supernatural creature that looks like a small person and enjoys causing trouble

hang (past **hung**) (v) kill someone by putting a rope around their neck and making them fall, used in some places and times to execute criminals

hive (n) a structure where bees live, here used to describe the house

howling (n) from verb **howl,** the long, loud sound that a dog or similar animal makes

in a jiffy PHRASE (usually spoken) very quickly or very soon

irrepressible (adj) impossible to control

jumble (n) a collection of different things mixed together

linger (v) stay a long time or take a long time to finish something

lull (n) a quiet period during an active situation

mare (n) an adult female horse

mastiff (n) a large, strong dog with short, smooth fur

mite (n) *quantifier*: a little bit

mitten (n) a type of glove with one part for your thumb and another part for your fingers

nook (n) a small corner or sheltered space

on the spot PHRASE immediately

pasture (n) land covered with grass where sheep, cows etc are kept

pious (adj) strict in your religious beliefs and practices

poker (n) a metal stick used for moving the coal or wood around on a fire

quaver (v) shake; if your voice quavers, it is not steady because you are feeling nervous or afraid

rap (n) a quick, hard hit, or the sound of this

rascal (n) a child who behaves badly but who you like too much to be angry with

rear (v) if an animal rears, it lifts its front legs up into the air

reign (n) the period of time when a king or queen rules a country

rough and tumble PHRASE play fighting but without anger or hurting each other

scorched (adj) burnt on the surface

scoured (adj) cleaned thoroughly by rubbing hard with something rough

scrub (n) a thorough wash or clean (more often used as a verb)

shaggy (adj) with long, thick and untidy hair

shingles (n) small flat pieces of wood like tiles that form the outer surface of a wall or roof

slap (n) a sharp hit with the palm of the hand

sled (see **sleigh**)

sleigh (n) (also **sled**) a vehicle sometimes pulled by animals and used for travelling over snow

smother laughter try to hide the sound of laughter

sniff (n) from verb **sniff**, smell something

snug (adj) if you are snug, you feel warm, comfortable and safe

sob (n) from verb **sob**, cry noisily while taking short breaths

stint (n) a period of time spent doing something

strike up (past **struck**) PHRASAL VERB start to play or sing a piece of music

sumptuous (adj) impressive, expensive and of high quality

swell (v) grow in size because of liquid collecting inside

to and fro PHRASE in one direction and then back again

tremble (n) shake especially because you are nervous, afraid or excited. If your voice trembles, you cannot talk in a steady, calm way.

tumble (v) if someone tumbles, they fall to the ground

undertaking (n) something difficult or complicated that you do

utter (adv) complete; often used for emphasizing how bad something is

wits (n) *plural*: your ability to think quickly and make sensible decisions

The Little Pies

accomplish (v) succeed in doing something, especially something that you have been trying to do for a period of time

amid (prep) with something all around you, here a smell

arouse (v) cause an emotion or attitude

artlessness (n) from adjective **artless**, very sincere and willing to trust other people

blow (n) a hard hit from someone's hand or an object

boulevard (n) *French*: a wide road in a town or city, often with trees along it

brandish (v) wave a weapon or other object around in your hand so that other people can see it

cane (n) a stick used for walking, often decorative

dilapidated (adj) a dilapidated building or vehicle is old and in bad condition

dismal (adj) making you feel unhappy

draw breath PHRASE temporarily stop doing something so that you can rest and breathe

gain (v) if a clock gains, it operates too fast

hag (n) *offensive:* an old woman who is ugly or unpleasant

haggard (adj) looking very tired, worried or ill

heron (n) a large bird with a long neck, long legs and a long, pointed beak that lives near water

languish (v) lose energy or become weak

mock (v) make someone look stupid by laughing at them

perspire (v) *formal*: sweat: produce liquid on your skin as a result of being hot, ill or nervous

puff (v) breathe noisily, especially because you have been running, climbing etc

quarter (n) a part of a town where you find particular buildings, activities or people

rustle (n) the sound made by the movement of leaves, paper etc

sidewalk (n) *US English*: a path with a hard surface beside a road. The British word is pavement.

spectacles (n) *plural, formal*: glasses that you wear to see

tremble (v) shake slightly

A Piece of Steak

adornment (n) decoration

apathetically (adv) not at all interested in or enthusiastic about anything

appalled (adj) offended or shocked very much by something, because it is extremely unpleasant or bad

aspiring (adj) hoping and trying to be successful at something, especially in your career

awe-stricken (adj) (normally **awe-struck**) feeling extremely impressed by something

bear a grudge (past **bore**) PHRASE continue to feel angry towards someone because they have done something to you that does not seem right or fair

bet (n) an agreement in which you predict what will happen and risk the loss of money if you are wrong, or stand to gain if you win

bitterness (n) a feeling of anger or unhappiness because of a bad experience, especially when you think that you have been treated unfairly

bluff (n) the act of deliberately giving a false idea to someone about the facts of a situation, especially in order to gain an advantage

bulk (n) something that is very large, wide and solid

bullock (n) a young male cow

cab (n) taxi

cherish (v) think that something is very important and wish to keep it

club (n) a thick, heavy stick used as a weapon

compel (v) force someone to do something

content himself (v) be willing to accept what you have, 'content to do' also possible

crouch (v) move your body close to the ground by bending your knees and leaning forwards slightly

cub (n) a young bear, lion, fox, wolf or other wild animal; here his children

cunning (adj) someone who is cunning uses their intelligence to get what they want

deft (adj) deft movements are made quickly and with skill

desert (v) if a feeling, quality or skill deserts you, you suddenly no longer have it

dizziness (n) the feeling as if you are spinning, especially when you think you are going to fall

dogged (adj) determined to achieve something and continuing to try despite difficulties

ebb (v) gradually become smaller or less

exultant (adj) *formal*: very pleased and excited, especially about something that you have achieved

falter (v) hesitate or stop speaking because you are nervous

flatterer (n) someone who praises another person in order to get what they want

game (adj) (used as an adverb in the story) prepared to join in with or try a difficult or dangerous activity

glance (v) look somewhere quickly and then look away

gnawing (adj) continuously causing you pain or worrying you

gravy (n) a sauce made from the juices of cooked meat thickened with flour

grin (v) smile showing your teeth

groggily (adv) from adjective **groggy**, feeling tired, weak or confused, especially because you are ill or have not had enough sleep

grope (v) try to get to a place by feeling the way with your hands

gruelling (adj) very difficult and involving a lot of continuous effort

harsh (adj) cruel, not soft or gentle

heyday (n) the period of time when a person, idea or object is most successful or popular

imperceptibly (adv) so slight or small that it is very difficult to notice

indignantly (adv) from adjective **indignant**, angry because of an unfair situation or someone's unfair behaviour

indubitably (adv) used for saying that something is certainly true

ineradicable (adj) not being able to remove something

inflict (v) cause something unpleasant to happen

insatiable (adj) always wanting more and never feeling satisfied

invariably (adv) always, or almost always

invincible (adj) too strong to be defeated

jarred (adj) shaken

laurels (n) *plural*: in sport, laurels are a recognition of achievement

lead (n) a very heavy, soft metal, chemical symbol Pb

loaf (v) spend time doing nothing

longing (n) a strong feeling of wanting someone or something

lose steam (past **lost**) PHRASE lose energy or enthusiasm

lose one's head (past **lost**) PHRASE stop thinking clearly or behaving in a sensible way

morosely (adv) feeling unhappy, in a bad mood and not wanting to talk to anyone

moulded (adj) given a particular shape

muffle (v) make less strong

mutter (v) talk in a quiet voice that is difficult to hear, especially because you are annoyed or are talking to yourself

on a hair trigger PHRASE needing only a slight influence to cause a reaction

outclassed (adj) be not as good as someone or something else

overwhelming (adj) from verb **overwhelm** beat someone or something because you are stronger than them

pandemonium (n) a very noisy and confused situation, especially one caused by a lot of excited people

pang (n) a very strong, sudden and unpleasant pain or emotion

pick (n) a tool used for breaking roads and other hard surfaces

recuperate (v) get better after being ill or injured

regardless (adj) without being affected or influenced by something

rigid (adj) stiff, hard and difficult to bend or move

scowl (n) an angry expression on someone's face

sheer (adj) used before noun for emphasizing the amount or degree of something: *sheer animal = all animal*

shovel (n) tool used for lifting soil, coal etc.

shrewd-faced (adj) looking able to judge people and situations very well and to make good decisions

spur (v) (or **spur on**) encourage someone to do something

stain (n) a mark left accidentally on clothes or surfaces

stake (n) something that you can keep or lose by taking a risk

stamina (n) the ability to work hard or exercise for a long time

steel yourself PHRASE prepare yourself for something unpleasant

strive (past **strove**) (v) to make a lot of effort to achieve something

superfluous (adj) not needed or wanted

toll (n) a payment, usually for using a bridge or road; here, the price that King pays is physical damage

trifle (n) *quantifier*: a little bit

unquenchable (adj) so strong that it cannot be satisfied, especially a thirst or desire

vigour (n) mental energy, enthusiasm and determination

wane (v) if a feeling or power wanes, it becomes weaker or less important

wary (adj) careful or nervous about someone or something because you think they might cause a problem

waver (v) if a person wavers, they are not certain about what to say or do

wear out (past **wore**) PHRASAL VERB use something a lot so that it gets old and no longer works

weary (adj) very tired, especially because of hard work or activity

whirlwind (adj) something that happens very quickly and unexpectedly

wistful pathos PHRASE a quality that makes you feel sorry for a person

weave (past **wove**) (v) make a cloth or fabric by placing threads around and on top of each other. Also used for movement: move around or between objects or people

wretchedness (n) terrible unhappiness

writhe (v) move by twisting and turning

yell (v) shout out in a loud voice because you are angry, afraid, excited or in pain

Like Water for Chocolate: January

archive (n) a place where you store historical documents and records

aside (n) a remark about something that is not the main subject of your discussion

attuned to PHRASE understanding and following a certain rhythm or routine that your are very familiar with

blast (n) a strong current of air, wind, heat etc

chill (n) a feeling of being cold

cower (v) move your body down and away from someone or something because you are frightened

dismantle (v) separate the parts of something

domain (n) an area of activity considered as belonging to or controlled by a particular person or group

draw water (past **drew**) PHRASE if you draw water you pull it up from an underground well

dribble (v) if a liquid dribbles, or if you dribble it, it flows slowly in small drops

expanse (n) a large area of land, water or sky

feign (v) pretend to have a particular feeling

flaw (n) a mistake or defect

gaze (n) someone's way of looking at someone or something

gingerly (adv) in a very slow and careful way, usually because you are injured or afraid of something

glee (n) a feeling of excitement and happiness that can include pleasure at someone else's bad luck

gossip (v) talk about other people or events

graze (v) touch or scrape lightly

grief (n) a strong feeling of sadness, usually because someone has died

happen to do something PHRASE do something by chance

hard of hearing PHRASE unable to hear well

have a say in something PHRASE if you have a say in something, you have the right to give your opinion and be involved in a discussion about it

hold/keep in check PHRASE control someone or something that might cause damage or harm

hollow (adj) empty inside

labour (n) the process by which a mother gives birth to a baby

liqueur (n) a sweet, strong alcoholic drink that you have at the end of a meal

lot in life PHRASE a person's quality of life, especially when it is determined by fate or luck

moisten (v) make something slightly wet

mourning (n) the process of expressing great sadness because someone has died

nausea (n) the feeling that you are going to vomit

prematurely (adv) *medical*: a premature baby is born before it should be

presumptuous (adj) showing too much confidence and not enough respect

pulse (v) if blood pulses, it flows with a strong regular movement caused by the heart beating

the recesses of PHRASE the parts of something that you cannot see easily because they are hidden or dark

remedy (n) a cure for pain or a minor illness

savour (v) enjoy the taste or smell of something as much as you can, often by eating or drinking it slowly

scrape off PHRASAL VERB to remove something by pulling a hard tool across the surface it is on

sear (v) burn the surface of something with extreme heat

slap (n) a sharp hit with the palm of the hand

spanking (n) (from verb **spank**) hit someone, especially a child, on their bottom with the palm of your hand

spring (past **sprang**) (v) used for saying that something is done quickly and with energy or force

stunned (adj) very shocked or upset, especially so that you are unable to act normally

swear (past **swore**) (v) make a sincere statement that you are telling the truth

trade (v) exchange something that you have for something else

uproar (n) a lot of very loud noise, made especially by people shouting

vigorous (adj) strong, active and healthy

vivid (adj) producing very clear and detailed images in the mind

vow (n) a serious promise

woozy (adj) *informal*: feeling slightly weak, confused and not very steady

A Piece of Pie

a month of Sundays PHRASE a very long time; normally in the negative expression: *never in a month of Sundays*

ale (n) a type of dark-coloured beer

an early grave PHRASE death before the natural age that you would expect

baffle (v) if something baffles you, you cannot understand it

break (n) an opportunity that helps you to be successful

brisk (adj) moving or acting quickly

bundle (n) a number of things that are loosely held together

consensus (n) agreement among all the people involved

distressing (adj) making you feel extremely unhappy, worried or upset

dressing (n) a mixture of liquids such as oil and vinegar that you pour over salad

emaciated (adj) extremely thin because of serious illness or lack of food

exploit (n) something unusual that someone does that you think is brave, exciting or entertaining

faint (n) a short time during which someone is unconscious

figure of speech PHRASE an expression in which the words are used figuratively, not in their normal literal meaning

frivolous (adj) silly, of no importance

green (adj) not experienced, especially because of being young

handicap (n) a disadvantage that prevents you from doing something well

hearsay (n) information that you have heard without having any proof that it is true

hearty (adj) friendly and enthusiastic

hiccough (also **hiccup**) (n) a short repeated sound that you make in your throat without intending to, usually because you have been eating or drinking too quickly

hostile (adj) very unfriendly or threatening

in your prime PHRASE if you are in your prime you are at the best or most successful stage in your life

indignation (n) anger about an unfair situation

indulge (v) have or eat something that you enjoy but that you should not have much of

jack pot (usually **jackpot**) (n) a large unexpected success or reward, here unusually referring to a competition

livelihood (n) something such as your work that provides the money that you need to live

manhole (n) a hole in a road or pavement, covered with a metal lid and used for entering an underground passage

My goodness gracious! PHRASE used for showing that you are very surprised, angry or upset. Often shortened to **Goodness!**

overtax (v) ask someone or something to make too large an effort so that they become very tired

phenomenal (adj) extremely impressive or surprising

pitiful (adj) looking or sounding so unhappy that people feel sympathy and sadness

place/put a premium on PHRASE believe that a particular quality or activity is very important

pleading (n) the act of asking for something in an urgent or emotional way

predicament (n) a difficult or unpleasant situation that is not easy to get out of

prosperous (adj) rich and successful

repulsive (adj) so unpleasant that you feel slightly ill when you see it

root (v) if you root for someone you support them in a game or sport often by cheering or applauding

running (adv) following one after another e.g. three months running = three months one following after another

school (v) train a horse so that someone can ride it, especially in competitions; here, train to win a competition

shrink (past **shrunk**) (v) become smaller in size

somewhat (adv) to some degree but not to a large degree

starch (n) a white substance without any taste that is found in rice, potatoes, and other vegetables. A type of carbohydrate that gives you energy.

startled (adj) suddenly frightened or surprised by something

stout (adj) slightly fat

substance (n) something with substance is big and heavy and takes up space

swivel (v) turn round on a fixed point and face in a different direction, here a noun meaning another look

tidbit (n) a small piece of food

turnstile (n) a narrow gate at an entrance gate with bars that move in a circle so that only one person at a time can go through

uneasiness (usually **unease**) (n) a feeling of being nervous, uncomfortable or unhappy about a situation

upshot (n) the result of a process or an event

waistband (n) the piece of cloth on a pair of trousers that goes round your waist

wedged (adj) fixed tightly or in a small space

zest (n) great enthusiasm or interest

Language study index

An Old-Fashioned Thanksgiving

Uses of *should*
Fronting as a literary device
Use of *but* for *except* and *instead*
Phrasal verbs

The Little Pies

Adding detail: participle clauses
Multiple-clause sentences

A Piece of Steak

The past perfect
Expressing regret
Quantifiers in collocations
Compound adjectives

Like Water for Chocolate: January

Colons and semi-colons
Common expressions

A Piece of Pie

Narrative tenses
Verb patterns

Visit the Macmillan Readers website at
www.macmillanenglish.com/readers

*to find **FREE resources** for use in class and for independent learning. Search our **online catalogue** to buy new Readers including **audio download** and **eBook** versions.*

Here's a taste of what's available:

For the classroom:

- **Tests** for most Readers to check understanding and monitor progress
- **Worksheets** for most Readers to explore language and themes
- **Listening worksheets** to practise extensive listening
- Worksheets to help prepare for the **First (FCE) reading exam**

Additional resources for students and independent learners:

- An **online level test** to identify reading level
- **Author information sheets** to provide in-depth biographical information about our Readers authors
- **Self-study worksheets** to help track and record your reading which can be used with any Reader
- Use our **creative writing worksheets** to help you write short stories, poetry and biographies
- Write academic essays and literary criticism confidently with the help of our **academic writing worksheets**
- Have fun completing our **webquests** and **projects** and learn more about the Reader you are studying
- Go backstage and read **interviews** with **famous authors** and **actors**
- Discuss your favourite Readers at the **Book Corner Club**

Visit** www.macmillanenglish.com/readers **to find out more!